Journey to Empowerment:
Tackling The Bullies Within

The experience of one woman who faced the most
despicable of human behaviour

Jacqueline A. Hinds

Disclaimer

The information contained in this book is for general information purposes only. The information is provided by Jacqueline A. Hinds and while we endeavour to keep the information up to date and correct, we make no representations or warranties of any kind, express or implied, about the completeness, accuracy, reliability, suitability or availability with respect to this publication or the information, products, services, or related graphics contained in this publication for any purpose. Any reliance you place on such information is therefore strictly at your own risk.

In no event will we be liable for any loss or damage including without limitation, indirect or consequential loss or damage, or any loss or damage whatsoever arising from loss of data or profits arising out of, or in connection with, the use of this publication.

Through this publication you are able to link to other resources and contacts which are not under the control of Jacqueline A. Hinds. We have no control over the nature, content and availability of those responsible for their management, operation or function. The inclusion of any links does not necessarily imply a recommendation or endorse the views expressed within them.

At the time of writing, every effort was made to keep the information in this publication current. However, Jacqueline A. Hinds takes no responsibility for, and will not be liable for, information being out of date or unavailable due to technical or any other issue beyond our control.

Contact Jacqueline A. Hinds at:
jah@wilsonhindsconsulting.com

"In life we need to be strong in the face of adversity and not lose sight of our life objectives or our goals; in order to be the success we were ordained to be"
Jacqueline A. Hinds

Dedicated

This book is dedicated firstly to **"Our Maker of Days"**, the one who truly stops us from falling; giving him all the glory and praise in seeing me through these trials and tribulations along this journey we call Life.

I also dedicate this book to my husband and my two children, I am feeling their love and feel truly blessed that they have supported me throughout this venture, giving me the time and space to put pen to paper.

Forever Blossom... My Inspiration

Jacqueline A. Hinds

Journey to Empowerment:
Tackling The Bullies Within

The experience of one woman who faced the most despicable of human behaviour

Contents

Acknowledgements   8

Foreword   9

About the Author – Jacqueline A Hinds   11

Introduction   15

Chapter 1 - The School Yard Bully   19

Chapter 2 - Should I Stay, or Should I Go?   25

Chapter 3 - A Steep Learning Curve   41

Chapter 4 - The Foundation Stone   53

Chapter 5 - The Phoenix Rising from the Ashes   67

Chapter 6 - Confidence Leads to Competence   83

Chapter 7 - As One Door Closed…   95

Chapter 8 - A Temporary Solution   115

Chapter 9 - After the Feast Came the Famine   123

Chapter 10 - Playing with the Big Boys   141

Chapter 11 - The Imperial Way   157

Chapter 12 - A Tripartite of Indifference   183

Chapter 13 - Full of Eastern Promise	219
My Journey to Empowerment	231
From a Thought Leaders' Perspective	234
Consultation Packages	243

Acknowledgements

I would like to thank everyone who supported me in bringing this book into being, from concept to fruition - a big thanks to my dear friends Marj and Amanda, who encouraged me; also to all those wonderful people who contributed by allowing me to highlight and share their thoughts, views and stories.

— ·· — ·· — ·· — ·· — ·· — ·· — ·· —

Lastly, I would like to thank those who were not so nice to me along my *Journey to Empowerment* thanking you because, without you, I would not have been passionate enough to pen this book; highlighting what really goes on within the arena of discrimination, inequality and biases. In doing so, I truly hope this book helps others along their own respective journey to empowerment.

"Your Journey is yours alone as
you travel this road we call Life,
others can walk it with you,
but no one can walk it for you"

Foreword

I first had the honour of meeting Jacqueline when she shared with me the bullying and discrimination she faced as a black woman in the NHS.

The challenges facing staff from black and minority ethnic backgrounds in the NHS and other public services are by now well recorded. We also now know that the opportunities to progress in the NHS are substantially less than for White staff and the treatment of BME is significantly worse.

Bullying, like discrimination, is insidious. It undermines confidence, erodes self-respect, impacts on one's loved ones and damages mental and physical wellbeing. We know that staff bullying in the NHS costs the organisation billions each year, adversely affecting patient care. Neither racism nor bullying are assaults on our humanity we should put up with and I know how hard it can be to stand against such treatment.

Jacqueline A. Hinds is a shining example of someone who has shown that despite the myriad of obstacles, it is possible to go forward, challenge racism and bullying, and develop the skills that can help others to do the same. Her story so far as told in this book, should encourage others very much so.

I commend it to you.

Roger Kline OBE
Research Fellow, Middlesex University
Trustee, Patient First UK

About the Author – Jacqueline A Hinds

Jacqueline A. Hinds is a Certified Emotional Intelligence Coach and Leadership Consultant. She's Board Chair & International Liaison for the Society of Emotional Intelligence, USA and Founder and Chair of the Society of Emotional Intelligence in the UK. She's passionate and dedicated in working with leaders and organisations helping them to understand and embrace the principles of Emotional and Cultural Intelligence; focusing on emotional resilience and inclusivity within the workplace and, Emotional Intelligence within Inclusive Leadership.

Jacqueline gained a wealth of knowledge and an impressive range of skills and experiences within various leadership positions across a range of high profile corporate organisations also, within the National Health Service (NHS). Throughout her career, she has always been on a learning curve, ensuring the knowledge gained is automatically shared, empowering others to develop and grow. While working, she gained a Master of Arts in Human Resource Development and her Post Graduate Diploma in Human Resource Strategies, using these skills to engage and work with organisations with a 'top down, bottom up' approach, thus enabling a (w)holistic and inclusive mindset and ethos when undertaking a range of organisational solutions, from transformational change, staff engagement to inclusion across the business arena.

Most recently, she has focused on building relationships within the Cybersecurity, Dementia Care and Education field, offering a range of interventions including Emotional and Cultural Intelligence Coaching for Leaders, inclusivity in the workplace and emotional resilience seminars and coaching, all delivered through her consultancy business Wilson Hinds Consulting Limited.

In her spare time, Jacqueline volunteers as a role model mentor with the Black Training Enterprise Group (BTEG) and is a participant on the Stephen Lawrence Charitable Trust's BAME Leadership Programme. She is running Emotional Resilience and Wellbeing workshops, supporting, motivating and empowering young men and women to be the best they can be as, they progress along their respective career pathways.

Having a strong faith, Jacqueline also runs a Woman of Faith Programme supporting women of all faiths. Women's

Ministries has always been her long-standing passion, and she feels blessed to be able to support these women of all denominations along their own walk of Faith through her ministering, coaching and fellowshipping.

She's currently writing her next book entitled *Supplements for the Soul*, an empowering and spiritual journey and walk of one's Faith.

Introduction

"Halcyon days... looking back and yearning for a glimpse of a time when things were simple and uncomplicated but Journey on, we must, fulfilling our destiny for...our footsteps have truly been ordered."
~ Jacqueline A. Hinds ~

I was inspired to write this book: *Journey to Empowerment: Tackling the Bullies Within*, because of my experiences along my educational and career history; which I must say, has been an incredible journey.

As longstanding and common threads, bullying, harassment and victimisation is perpetuated throughout organisations across the globe. There has been and continues to be, much talk of initiating training that raises awareness about unconscious bias and racism and, more to the point, how these should be tackled in the workplace. Yet, unfortunately that is just it - talk.

I grew up in a small multicultural rural town, where, in that time there was news of black people being abused. Once, there was talk at school about a group of skinheads who targeted black men for having relationships with white women. My older brother, for example, and his now wife were subjected to this behaviour when they started dating at school.

Discrimination and racism were spoken about in our home and my mother often told me stories about her up-close-and-personal experiences when she first arrived to live in the UK. Almost like a parable, these experiences were shared with me but, not in great detail by either my mother or father. I suppose they did like so many other parents from the Caribbean, who had similar experiences at the time. Yet, nothing was really done by them to confront the perpetrators or the system, unless it was very necessary for them to do so. Instead, their solution was to keep their head down and "get on with it".

I talk about my journey to empowerment, because it truly has been a *journey to my empowerment*; from where I felt bullied in the school yard through to my experiences in the corporate and public sectors. It has been over 30+ years since I have left school, venturing into the working world and gaining invaluable knowledge, skills and experiences; which at times, had been soul-destroying and often filled with a variety of trials and tribulations. Yet, I overcame the many barriers I faced and, by channeling my loneliness, hurt and anger, I was able to support others in a positive and meaningful way. Eventually, I learnt how to lend that experience to those who were being bullied or harassed; often willing them to rise up and fight against the injustices meted out to them. Even so, it was not easy for them to do, since it probably was not in their nature - very much like our parents before us.

As I took on more roles, I decided I wanted to become a Human Resource Development specialist, where I would be in a better position to combat and confront this abhorrent behaviour. I knew there were people who were unaware of their rights as an employee or even conversant with the relevant policies and procedures that could be used to strengthen their position. Yet, as I progressed in my own career, the training and coaching I received, increased my knowledge-base and experience and, as a result, I have facilitated stress-related workshops and career coaching sessions, helping individuals seeking support to transition out of their current role into a new job or career.

In my professional career, I was subjected to discrimination, bullying, undermining and other forms of exclusion and, there were times when things got so bad, I nearly gave up and moved on, which would have been exactly what the bullies wanted. But instead, I reacted by focusing on my successes whether big or small, and these enabled me to overcome the challenges I faced. *Journey to Empowerment: Tackling the Bullies Within* shares my highs and downright devastating lows, and how I tackled these bullies. This book is by no means a boo hoo sob story, but more like a look-at-what-happened-to-me-and-I-overcame-it kind of book; providing readers with an insight into the affect and effect bullying has on an individual, debilitating them and rendering them incapable of going forward or backward in their career. Yet, humour inhabits this book too, and anyone who knows me, knows I like a good laugh. Sometimes, that was what was needed in some situations and, just like what my mother used to say...*you've got to sometimes take bad things and laugh!* This was so true. I have poured my whole being into this book and hope you the reader, will gain some nuggets of knowledge and encouragement to support you along your own journey.

> *"I can't take your journey for you, but I can promise you one thing, I'll be there to keep you company along the way."*

Jacqueline A. Hinds

Chapter 1 - The School Yard Bully

"Turn your wounds into Wisdom"
~ Oprah Winfrey ~

The first time I realised I was actually being bullied was when I was in secondary school and, back then, the bullying stemmed more from rivalry than anything else. Even the teachers were trying to outdo each other, presenting a top student in their class and form group as 'the one' surpassing all others.

In my situation, my bully or nemesis was goaded on by others in her form group; especially those wanting to stir the pot by picking fights with individuals just to ascertain how 'hard' a person was. Back then, there were girl and boy gangs but, the girl gangs seemed to be more prevalent - for some reason. They would give each other signature names taken from the most popular television programmes of the time and Charlies Angels was one such classic, where the lead characters' names were used i.e. Sabrina, Kelly and Jill - and the girls would try and act just as badass as these women in the school yard. They would never use or call each other by their birth names and even re-enacted the fight scenes. It was their way of flexing their muscles, letting everyone know who was in charge. This type of bullying happened all the time at school and there was one particular incident that occurred between me and the lead bully. It happened after our school sports day.

We competed against each other in various events and the competition between us was tight; we matched each other in strength and every ability. The only thing, we were on opposing sides, not only in sports but in academia as well as we were split into two streams (7RN and 7BT), and always came to a head-to-head.

That school year, the classes had more than one teacher for the same subject as well as aligned to one of the two-year groups. My typing tutor for my year group (forgot her name) was really nice and supportive. The other year group had Mrs. Morgan. Funnily enough, I remembered her name and not that of my own typing tutor. Think of it this way, you always recalled the name of the person who either hurt or was horrible to you!

Both tutors had a serious competitive streak between them, and it seemed the rivalry emanated more from Mrs. Morgan than my own teacher. I guess it was because of her length of service and seniority, in comparison to my younger tutor. Between them, they often talked about which girls were at the top of their class and would compare notes such as typing speeds and accuracy, especially after mock tests. This reminded me so much of high-profile horse trainers (not that I considered myself or anyone else of being a horse), who were dedicated in training their prize thoroughbreds to outperform each other. There was one particular occasion, when the Head of Year had made some negative comments, probably a bit too loud to another teacher, about a couple of students. Some pupils nearby overheard, but what could they do? I would say that bullying was definitely rife there, from the top to the bottom.

In my incident, it started off as harmless banter between another student and I, about who was better at whatever. Eventually, it became a bit more serious, where point scoring and pole positioning was at the forefront of our minds; with being number one, the ultimate goal. Our harmless comments progressed to name calling before finally coming to an all out-and-out showdown. It was in the common room, where after throwing a few citrus peels at me, she called me out.

I quietly sat minding my own business, reading a book when the peels came at me. Flanked by her crew, like bodyguards, she prodded and cajoled me. This type of bullying was totally different to what my older siblings used to do. In fact, it was much worse. At least with my siblings I fought back, but here in school, it was like being in a cage fight with eager spectators looking on, waiting for a good show. But I was not going to lower myself. Why? So that someone could say: *"You're hard. You can fight."* I was determined I was not going to play that game, so I ignored the peels flying in my direction and her crew's catcalls, spurring her to challenge me: *"Come on outside if you think you're hard."*

Word got around the school about an imminent fight and more kids came looking for some action. Although I felt scared, I decided I was not going to show any fear and tried to carry on reading, regardless of the commotion going on around me. That was when a large piece of peel hit me square on my forehead. I felt the anger rise within me as I stared at her, but my instinct kicked in. I was ready to fight but did not want to start it. Suddenly, something else happened as I looked at the sea of faces, eagerly waiting for the bust-up to begin. Anyone would have thought that it was a big boxing gala night with both opponents waiting for the bell. Yet, as fast as the anger pilot fight light was lit within me, it was extinguished. I had a thought. We had not argued, and there were no incidents I could recall where we actually had. Fact of the matter was, I never really wanted to fight. After all, I had nothing against her and calmly said, "I do not want to fight you but if you still want to fight you can...on one condition...you throw the first punch. I'll then finish it!"

I was just as surprised as she was at my statement, but I had made up my mind that I had nothing to lose and, wherever that bravado came from I really did not know. She needed to throw that first punch. Yes, she probably would have beaten me, but I was adamant I was not going to comply and give them a good show. Funnily enough, she did not throw a punch and just proceeded to call me all sorts of names as she tried intimidating and provoking me. Her efforts were in vain, though, as I had completely taken control of my emotions, calming right down, outing the flame altogether.

This was my victory I was not bothered about what anyone else felt regardless of what they called me. I knew I had not given the bully and her cronies what they wanted. **On that day, I had learnt a valuable lesson and more to the point, this lesson was to be recalled on numerous occasions,**

helping me throughout my career journey. It was then I realised that bullies only had power if you relinquished and gave them your own. I say, do not do it. Be your authentic self. Stand your ground. I know it may not be easy, but it was achievable.

Now, whenever my thoughts drift back to those school days, I acknowledge that some of us may have been subjected to bullying, witnessed someone being bullied or even dare I say, were the actual school yard bully. Today, some individuals do not realise that they are being bullied; accepting how they are treated as a way of life, hoping things would get better whenever they moved to senior school, college, university or even work. But, within their psyche, a pattern of acceptance may have emerged.

There was a saying - bullies never prosper - and in reality, they never do, since that feeling of being almighty by making someone else feel small and insignificant tended to be short-lived. A bully needed to continue feeding this arrogant mannerism in order to maintain their position and in all honesty, it said a lot about them as an individual, more so than the person they are bullying.

Chapter 2 - Should I Stay, or Should I Go?

*"It's not hard to make decisions
once you know what your values are."*
~ Roy E. Disney ~

I never mentioned any of the bullying incidents to my parents since it was more trouble than it was worth. We lived in a small town and a close community, where the parents knew and worked with each other. So, I would have probably ended getting into trouble even though it was not my fault. The least said, the better. As children, we just got on with it, kids were fighting all the time and, it was not as if I could not defend myself. After all, I fought with my siblings and thus learnt to defend myself and, unless it was a life-threatening situation, I would not bother my parents. Eventually, I just saw it as my secondary school journey.

I was the third eldest and with the best will in the world, my parents were supportive and wanted the best for me and my five siblings. As parents, they were busy working and like many of the children at my school whose parents were in the same position. They were like ships passing in the night, since my mother worked nights in a maternity hospital and my father worked in a large foundry, during the day. It was my mother, like many other mothers, who was seen as the one who dealt with my schooling, being more involved than my father; especially when it came to Parent's Evening or something had happened.

In one incident, my Head of Year felt the need to call my mother to tell her that I was improperly attired by not wearing the proper school uniform. Normally, you were told off and maybe a letter was sent to your home, but not on this occasion. I do not know why it happened the way it had, but it happened giving me a glimpse into how someone could use their position and power to make an example of someone else. I actually felt sorry for the Head of Year, but I was the child and the one in trouble.

In those days there were fashion fads and I know some of you would remember…*Sunray pleated skirts*! They were skirts worn down to the ankle and the look was complemented with a pair of Kickers® or 'Earthman's' - preferably suede. My Head of Year called me out as I headed to a lesson, she was at one end of a corridor and I, at the other. She shouted that I was not wearing the right school uniform and there I was thinking she was colourblind as I could not figure out how she saw it was a blue and not a black skirt from where she stood. Yet, she instructed me to go and wait in her office. Oh yes, I forgot to mention…I did not actually own a Sunray-pleated skirt, the one I wore I had "borrowed" from my Mum's wardrobe.

I did as I was told and waited outside the office door. When she arrived, I was ordered to sit on the chair opposite her desk, she then proceeded to tell me off. At that point, I felt she wanted to make an example of me since it was the second time I had been in this situation. The first time was when I 'bunked off' from school – but that is a story for another day! She asked if I had anything to say before she called my mother, I pleaded and asked her not to, explaining that my Mum worked nights and would be asleep. She ignored me and dialled my home number. When my mother picked up and answered the phone, I knew she was annoyed, after all, her sleep was now broken. The Head of Year launched into a dialogue about why she was calling and, when she was finished my mother asked if that was why she had called. My mother then explained that unless it was a matter of life or death, the Head of Year should never ring her again as she worked nights. At that moment and after my mother unceremoniously put the phone down on her, I witnessed the startled look on my Head of Year's face. I also knew I was in for the *'high jump'* when I got home; one, for taking her skirt and two, the phone call from my school. To make matters worse, I received detention for the whole week. I guess the Head of Year had been made to feel humiliated by my mother.

After my bullying incident, my time at school passed relatively easy. Not that the bully and I became the best of buddies or anything like that, but something had changed after that day in the common room. There were no longer any challenges or orange peels thrown my way. In fact, we became regular pupils, displaying great sportsmanship and camaraderie as we competed against each other. Yet, in participating in the various events and, at such young ages, we operated with such professionalism I hadn't realised either one of us possessed.

I did, however, start to see other people being bullied by other pupils and teachers, and it seemed a normal way of life. Although I was glad I was no longer on the receiving end, I knew what that person was going through and felt helpless, unable to do anything. I knew that if I had tried to step in, I would be on the radar of the bullies, facing the same treatment. In the same breath, I really empathised with those pupils who were being bullied, sometimes being cornered in the playground where no teachers were present, a helpless and resigned look on their faces and in their body language, showing they had given up. I would look at them, trying to make eye contact, silently urging them to fight back, not physically but with a confidence and determination to overcome this form of victimisation. But not everyone had the confidence I had to stand up to bullying; believe me, it was sometimes a very lonely road to travel.

By the end of 1980 and the school year, I had progressed very well with my typing tutor – that was what happened when you learned to touch type at ten-years-old! At that age, my mother had decided it would be a good idea if I learnt how to touch-type as she felt the skills I would gain, would put me in good stead for jobs later on in my career.

My tutor would set regular typing tests between Mrs. Morgan's star pupil and I and, there were times I felt really embarrassed, feeling somewhat like a prized possession being paraded in front of the other students, especially when I had scored higher than anyone else. I would picture both teachers in the staff room, conversing and comparing scores on what their star pupil had attained. Imagine the smugness from one whose pupil had scored the highest! Yet, all of this was about to come to an end as decisions were being made without my knowledge and I, too, had decisions to make about what I wanted to do when I left school and with my eventual career. The news came before our final typing exams.

I was taking extra classes to brush up on my typing speed and accuracy, since I would be tested by the Royal Society of Arts (RSA) Levels I and II and was expecting really good grades in the exams. I had also decided that when I finally left school, I wanted to be a court stenographer. I was not sure what qualifications I needed but, fancied myself sitting there taking notes on that tiny stenograph machine. If that failed to transpire, I was already fully equipped to do a secretarial role. So, I attended a series of lessons through the Scheidegger Typing Institute, paid for by my mum. At first, I disliked the lessons but as my confidence grew so did my enthusiasm, speed and eventually, I learnt to touch-type without looking at the keyboard.

My mother wanted me to work in an office, so it was a difficult conversation I had with her when I informed her, I was not staying on for sixth form. She could not understand how a teacher could have caused me not to stay, but I explained to her how I felt, especially with the fact that the tutor did not really like me. I told her that I wanted to experience the real world and gain experience that way. She totally understood, and we never spoke about it again which was a relief. Since my father left everything to my mother, my two older brothers had little to say since they were in college and working. As for my three younger siblings, they were still in school so did not feature in the conversations. I thought about going to college, then getting a job as I really could not see myself even going to university and to be honest, I was not really keen on going there either but knew I needed to study in order to achieve my goals and aspirations.

This decision came about while I was determining where my experience and qualifications could take me in my career, whether in the courts or elsewhere. But once I had finished sixth form, I thought about staying on and that changed when my teacher dropped her bombshell.

It was while talking to her about staying on, I asked what I could expect under her tutelage. She encouraged me to stay on and told me about the benefits of gaining the necessary qualifications I needed. Then, suddenly she told me that she was returning to South Africa – the land of her birth. I was shocked. This was the one person who had encouraged me to be all I could be and, if she was not going to be my tutor, I knew who would be. Just the thought was enough for me, and it was then that I decided I would be leaving school altogether and going straight into a job.

Needless-to-say, I had my exams and came away with Distinctions at both levels. I was very pleased but sad that my teacher was leaving, and Mrs. Morgan would have ended up been my tutor, and I knew how she could make my life miserable by chipping away at my confidence. I also knew I would have been subjected to some form of bullying since her star pupil was also staying on for further education. As the only typing tutor remaining in the school, Mrs. Morgan would have ensured her star pupil always had everything she needed, including assistance in her career choice.

Once, my tutor had sent me to ask Mrs. Morgan for some replacement typing ribbons and correction fluid. It was like

Oliver going up to the schoolmaster and asking for more gruel. Her response made me feel second class. She had never been civil towards me and whenever I did better than her star pupil, there was always an indifference in her behaviour whenever we interacted.

Although, I was indecisive as to whether I would stay or leave school, I knew I could not stay for sixth form. It was crystal clear after my teacher said she was leaving, and this became the crucial deciding factor that led me to have the conversation with my mother and, though she was a little disappointed, she had accepted my decision.

Out There in the World

I left school at sixteen. Leaving with enough qualifications for me to get my first job - a six-month work experience in a small printing and plumbing firm. A strange business combination but it worked. There were two directors and one secretary and now me, the newest addition to the team as the junior/copy typist. This role provided me with the grounding on how to work in any office environment, but looking back, I would say I was bullied by the senior secretary but not realising it at the time. Even so, the knowledge and skills I gained were invaluable as were the lessons about bullying. It came in various forms and being fresh out of school I accepted the treatment as I did not know any better. All I knew was that I was there to learn, so it never entered my mind about being bullied, especially since all I knew about bullying was what I had left behind in the school yard.

Each day I was busy, and not just with typing letters, answering the phone or taking messages. As soon as I arrived at work, I would wash the day-before-dirty mugs, then made the directors their special blend of coffee and the senior secretary, her cup of tea. This was my "Rites of Passage" and because it was a plumbing and printing firm, there were queries and stocktaking, both laborious and backbreaking. In addition to these tasks, I had to climb a ladder and fill shelves with stock, but the task I really detested, was the large reports and documents that needed to be done on a Banda machine and produced in triplicate. Every time a report was created and needed to be amended, I was the one who ended up doing it. The senior secretary always making sure ample supplies of white, blue and pink correction fluid were available. This precious liquid was essential to amend each copy of the triplicate report with the right colour. It annoyed me as I was never given the opportunity to type a report but was always expected to do the corrections and this would take hours.

There were many times I wanted to retaliate, especially when I was being ordered around and given the menial tasks to do. I knew I was there to learn but I hardly had time to catch my breath before there was another task to do. Yet, I did not say anything, because I knew I was only there for a short time and just wanted the experience plus, I was losing weight since I never kept still! Even when there was nothing to do, the senior secretary would have me doing all sorts of office jobs, even if the task had already been completed. I would work from the time I arrived until I left to go home, once I was home, I would just fall asleep!

That transition from school to the world of work was not an easy one and, diving straight into a 9 to 5 job was one of the toughest lessons I learnt as a sixteen-year old. After I had finished my work experience, I thought it would be easy to get a job as a copy typist. I wrote a well-crafted cover letter, enclosed with my resume and sent to as many organisations in and around my hometown. I was hopeful and confident that my qualifications and work experience would open doors for me - how wrong was I!

I sent out so many and received just as many rejections. It was soul-destroying. I was so convinced I was going to get at least one or two interviews, where they would test my typing skills and I would then be offered a job. But I became disillusioned. I had the skills and just wanted an opportunity to show how competent I was. Weeks went by and still the rejection letters came, and I placed these in chronological order in a box file I kept. I felt so helpless, frustrated and angry but I did not stop and soon started looking in other areas before finally doing archaeology by joining a dig and working part-time in our local museum. I always had a love for archaeology, so this was a lovely distraction for me.

Eventually, though, I secured a role as a security ledger clerk in an organisation that supplied pool tables and fruit machines to pubs and clubs. I enjoyed the job but there was one thing I was not too keen on as it entailed figure work, and to be honest, mathematics was not one of my favourite subjects at school. I would have left the job a lot sooner but, it gave me an opportunity to keep up with my typing skills. Each ledger officer worked with the security officers and as part of their role they needed to type and present a weekly report. There was one security officer in particular, who absolutely abhorred typing and on hearing this, I approached him and offered to type his reports for him. He gratefully accepted, giving me the much-needed experience, I craved in order to maintain my typing speed and accuracy.

I then began to think about my next move and fancied working in a bank. I suppose it was the professional look that appealed to me and this was the benchmark I had set myself. So, I stayed in my current role for a year, before deciding to go further afield by applying for jobs in London. My younger sister was doing so too since she was applying to study nursing.

It happened that we had our interviews on the same day and so we travelled to London. I was in the City and she was at a hospital in North West London. My interview was at a clearing bank in Moorgate. I was nervous as I arrived and asked for Sandra Funk, the recruitment officer. She interviewed me and said my typing was to be tested on a golf-ball typewriter! The thing was I had never used one before let alone seen one as I had learnt to type on a manual typewriter. So here I was, about to do a typing test on a completely new typewriter I had never used before. I was apprehensive. When I finished the test, Sandra looked at the passage and said I had gone over the five-error mark that was allowed and any errors over this amount resulted in the individual being rejected. I was crestfallen. I guess it showed since Sandra said that the passage, I had just typed was perfectly neat and paginated, barring the errors. She then said something I never forgot: "You've come all of this way and I don't want you to go home only for us to call you back to redo the test. Do you want to do it again?"

Having a better handle on the golf-ball typewriter and being much calmer, I retyped the test - and passed! I got a lucky break that day. Sandra had seen the potential in me, and I was able to secure the job. This opportunity also took me into the bright lights of the big city of London – a place where my real Journey to Empowerment was about to begin.

I began to gain a lot of insight into human nature and behaviour as I began tapping into my emotional intelligence by watching other people's body language, picking up their signs as they interacted with me or with each other. Although I was still young, this knowledge proved useful in the future. Having left school at sixteen, the experiences I gained in my first job put me in good stead for my next role and although archaeology was not secretarial work, it too gave me the skills to engage with people from all levels and walks of life. That was invaluable. And who knows, if I had fallen out of love with being a secretary, I could have been an archaeologist. I suppose this could have been my backup career.

Country Girl comes to Town!

Chapter 3 - A Steep Learning Curve

"I've learnt in life, that you can still keep growing in knowledge and experience achieving your goals and aspirations; even when the odds are stacked against you and the outlook seems grim."
~ Jacqueline A. Hinds ~

So here I was, my first day in my new job, in London! I was excited, apprehensive and nauseous. I was travelling on a steam train – yes, a steam train - from Bedford to St Pancras Station and as this was my first job away from home, I felt so lost in the sea of moving people. I had never worked in London before even though I had visited on numerous occasions but that was mostly to party or go clubbing and even then, someone usually drove me and my friends there and back. So, we never caught the train. Yet, here I was, going somewhere I was unfamiliar with, and finding out I was unable to navigate London Underground. When I looked at the Tube Map, I felt so helpless because I could not understand it. To me, it looked all over the place. And, even though, I had a welcome letter with the bank's address on it, I still had no clue as to how I was going to get there, I was distraught.

While at the station as time ticked away, I plucked up the courage and approached a male station attendant and asked him how I could get to the bank's address. I explained to him it was my first time travelling on London's underground and had no idea on how to navigate it. He took me down into the underground, showed me which line to take and said when I reached my destination station, I should ask for directions. It was a traumatic trip. I nearly bawled my eyes out a couple of times because I was confused and even with his help, I still managed to get on the wrong train. I totally hated being in that confined space with so many people. Finally, though, I was standing in front of the office, arriving on time but…wow…what a journey!

The head office was a magnificent building with its beautiful architecture and ornate fittings; I was collected from reception by a young lady. As we walked through the long corridors, she did not converse with me and that made me even more nervous. There was no warmth in her greeting or introduction either, not that I expected to be welcomed with open arms or anything like that but, a pleasant hello would have been enough.

She told me I would be working as a junior secretary in the Planning Department. I knew that but said nothing since it was already written in my offer letter. We reached the fifth floor, walked in and I was shown my desk. I felt all eyes were on me as I walked in and noticed she failed to introduce me to anyone; nobody came and said hello either. Eventually, she said, "Here you are, you'll be working here at this desk." Then promptly left.

I waited for a few minutes before she returned with my boss. He said he was the Director of the Planning Department and hoped I would be happy working there. To be honest I could not remember what I said or how the first day went since it went so fast. I could not even remember the journey back to St. Pancras Station or getting the train home. Later on, in my life, whenever I spoke about my journey to work, many people seemed really intrigued when I told them I had travelled on a steam train for my first job. More often than not, they would enquire how old I was! Back then, the train line was known as the BedPan Line – funny that - and its real name was the Bedford to St Pancras Line.

Each day after, I would leave early and by the end of the first week one would have thought I had been travelling to and from London all my working life. Whenever I got into work each morning, I greeted the receptionists, showed my ID to security and went to my floor; there I would greet my colleagues. Though they were pleasant I never felt any warmth from them I was unsure if it was because I was the only Black person working there. It seemed that they had a problem communicating with me and, at the time, I put it down to being the new girl but on reflection, I knew it was because I was Black. It was not anything that was said or done, it was just how they interacted differently with me than with each other.

In the early 1980's, the bank made a series of acquisitions and it was the department's role to ensure that the offices were refurbished. There was plenty of work for all the secretaries and when I arrived at work every day, I would be greeted with a filing tray full of reports, letters and documents to be typed, amended and delivered before the end of the day. And each evening whenever I returned home, I would tell my mother about my day and the way I felt I was being treated. I told her about when I went for lunch, the other secretaries would eat elsewhere. My mother encouraged me to tough it out since the role and opportunity did not come around that often and it would help get me to where I really wanted and needed to be.

Although I enjoyed the job, I really felt uncomfortable. I felt my colleagues were not used to working with me or never attended a school where there were Black people. Sometimes, it felt awkward as if they were uncertain of what to say, always asking me how I liked working there. In truth, it felt like I was the 'hired help' since the work I was given was uninteresting, while the stimulating tasks were being done by the other junior secretaries. It felt as if everyone had a fully filled plate and I, the scraps. It was no wonder that I became bored and felt I needed to consistently wear a façade to "fit in", almost like wearing a pair of shoes that actually did not fit.

And whenever I spoke to the other secretaries it felt like I needed to speak and behave in a certain manner for them to interact with me. Even then, it needed to be something that they were interested in or could relate to like a pop band on the charts. If one of the secretaries asked anything personal, I would politely respond because I knew they were not really interested. After which, there would be no further conversation. Awkward! It was as if they were merely on a fact-finding mission and once they found out what they needed to know, that was it. Even when making tea or coffee, they rarely asked if I wanted a cup. I think they actually felt that as the new girl, I should be the one making it for them. So, I would make my own coffee.

While working there I never actually made any friends. Sure, initially, they had shown me where they went for lunch, with me tagging along a couple of times but I think they were only being civil, showing me where to eat. So, after a couple of weeks, I got my own lunch, finding a place in the staff restaurant or eat at my desk with a book or magazine. It was a lonely road to travel day-in-day-out, but I had no choice. I decided to overcome their indifference by just getting on with my work and wearing my "mask". Although I disliked the façade, it was required. I was in the City of London and needed to get on with my colleagues, gaining the knowledge of the culture and environment I was working in. Eventually, I became tired of doing this, as it took more effort to keep up the façade than to be my authentic self. Yet, being polite and just "getting on with it", was about to change for me and become the turning point in my career; leading me down the learning and development pathway.

It was just before Christmas and tradition had it that an invite was sent to all staff members from their immediate boss – in this case the Director - inviting us into his office for a pre-Christmas drink. By then, I had been in the department for about one month and did not think the invitation was meant for me being the newest member of the team. But it was, and at the insistence of the senior secretary, I had to go. Once there, the director opened his drinks cupboard - a standard piece of office furniture for senior leadership – and asked everyone what they would like to drink. It was the first time I saw *"servant leadership"* in action. I laugh at this particular memory since I was not accustomed to drinking, although I partied and clubbed. I also did not want to be the odd one out, so I listened to what everyone ordered and most asked for Gin and Tonic. When it was my turn, I spoke with a level of confidence and asked for the same tipple, like I was a seasoned drinker. I took a little sip and gagged, trying hard to hold it together. I absolutely hated it but it was my fault. I could have asked for orange, pineapple or tomato juice but no - Miss-I-Do-Not-Want-To-Be-The-Odd-One-Out - decided to go for Gin and Tonic. With everyone watching I had no choice but to drink it, taking small sips, whilst trying to make idle talk.

Before the soiree concluded the executive assistant to the managing director approached me and asked that I stayed behind after everyone had left. Apparently, he wished to have a word with me. I was quite chilled and that was probably down to the Gin and Tonic. Still, I was keen to hear what they had to say and in a funny way, I knew exactly what that was going to be.

Finally, the director, executive assistant and I were the only ones left. The executive assistant took the lead and asked me how I was liking the job and whether I was happy doing what I was doing. I thought this was a bit odd, but said I liked the job. She gave no indication as to where the conversation was going but I felt there was something they wanted from me. She asked other questions which I thought made no sense, and then asked me if I had considered any other roles in the organisation that I had thought of doing or, if there was anywhere else in the bank I thought of working. Alarm bells rang in my head. The department was quite structured, the work repetitive and a little boring but I could not believe what I was hearing, they were actually asking, in a roundabout way, if I minded moving to a different section, using the busyness of the department and repetition of the work as an excuse to do so.

To be honest, I was relieved, because I was unsure of how long I could have kept up the façade, working with people who I knew disliked me. I asked what other departments or roles they felt I was suited for. The executive assistant mentioned the bank's training centre near St. Pancras Station as a suitable place where I could "fit" in better. She must have figured I had been lonely and needed to be in an environment where I could easily interact with other staff members. The director then said he knew I would like it at the training centre, since the work there was more varied than in the planning department. He also said that there were a lot more people there my age too. I thought that was nice for him to say and I said I would be interested. At that point, the executive assistant said she would contact them to see when I could move over. As I listened, it was difficult to gauge how they truly felt about the situation but, nonetheless, it was good news for me.

When I re-entered the office, it was quiet and I noticed a few people whispering with each other as I made my way back to my desk. No one said anything to me, but I felt they knew all about the conversation I had just had. Later on, I noticed a difference in my colleagues' behaviour towards me. They were much friendlier than usual, even conversing with me a lot more. It could have been my imagination, or they were just happy to know I was leaving. To that thought, I would never know.

Christmas came and went and in early January I received a letter stating I had been offered a role in the training centre, working for the administration manager. I was to join by the end of the month. By that time, I had been in the planning department for nearly three months. I was moving to a new role, a five-minute walk down the road from the station I arrived at every morning. I was not apprehensive about it either, since I was hopeful it would be a lot more real, where people actually talked with each other about everything and not just about work. The planning department felt sterile and devoid of any emotion and there were times I felt like I was a robot – I arrived, worked, finished, then went home.

Looking back, I saw the difference in working for a large organisation and its culture as opposed to being in a smaller one. I had not known what to expect but realised it had been a steep learning curve and I quickly learnt how to create a façade, adapting to blend in. I had felt bad not being my authentic self but understood that I was in unchartered territory and needed to play the game in order to survive. Since I was just starting out and wanted to progress, the will to survive in this corporate arena was far greater than anything else. So, here I was about to move into another role, unsure of what to expect but was forever grateful of the opportunities and the experiences I had gained thus far.

Chapter 4 - The Foundation Stone

*"One has to remember that every failure can
be a stepping-stone to something better."*
~ Colonel Sanders ~

The day finally arrived. I was starting my new role. My job: Copy Typist to the Administration Manager. This sounded a little bit elevated in status than just being a copy typist but...it was right next to the Administration Manager and it could not get any bigger than that!

I arrived at St. Pancras on a crisp January morning and thought, what was it going to be like in this new role? Would I enjoy it there? Would my colleagues like me? I silenced the noise. My head and heart were having a conversation about how they thought my first day would pan out; not arguing with each other but more curious than anything. I really wanted to just get there and get on with my new job.

With my departure from the planning department the week before went so fast, I was relieved. Now I was excited. My time at the department had taken over my whole-being and I was moving with a clearer mindset, into how I was going to navigate my career from now on. Do not get me wrong, I learnt a lot during my time in the planning department but in all honesty, it was not coded into my DNA to work in an environment where I felt like a robot. I suppose it was a bit young and naïve of me to really think that everything was going to be great and people would be friendly and ultimately, I would be happy from then on. But I had no benchmark to compare the experience to, so, I probably set my hopes a bit too high and when reality finally hit, it was a bit painful.

I came out of St. Pancras and walked in the direction of Pentonville Road, so differently than navigating my way to the Northern Line, taking me to the Head Office. Yes, the hustle and bustle of people going about their business, trying to get to work was still there but there was also a different feeling. I was elated and as I walked, I made a mental note of all the eateries and clothes shops along the way. There was so much to see leading up to my new place of work that I felt so relaxed. Everybody looked normal - I know that sounds silly but it was unlike working in the City. Essentially, the people in the office and pedestrians I saw looked at ease with themselves and not stiff! Immediately I felt at home! How could I feel at home and I had not even started working as yet? In my whole being I felt an overwhelming feeling that I was going to be okay; it was as if I knew I was going to enjoy this job.

Welcome to Webb House

I arrived at Webb House and walked to the main doorway, where there were two entrances. I double-checked the numbers and went through the doorway that had the bank's symbol etched on a silver plaque next to it and headed to reception. A couple of men sat on reception, both wearing dark grey suits. I later found out that their roles were multifaceted, and they did doing far more than just issue badges and escort visitors. I signed the visitor's book as a new employee and was told to return later that day for my staff ID badge. One of the men took me to the administration office via a lift to the third floor. In the lift it was strange because I could not see a first or second floor button on the control panel. There were just floors three to six. Later, I found out that part of the ground floor - the other entrance doorway – was where the first and second floors of Webb House were located, and where British United Provident Association (BUPA), an international healthcare group, was situated.

In the administration office I was introduced to Joanne, the assistant administration manager. She welcomed me, then introduced me to the team. Seated at their desks and in a horseshoe shape, were eight members of staff; the assistant administration manager's desk, at the top, facing them. After the introductions, Joanne, took me to the office where I would be located and there, I was introduced to my new boss and three secretaries who were part of the typing pool. They were using word processors – called Wang... well, that's what they were called back then. Two of the secretaries smiled at me and one introduced herself as the Principal Secretary. She seemed pleasant enough, but there was something about her that so reminded me of some of the people I had worked with in the office I had just left. I shrugged that feeling off, but it was to return, revisiting me quite frequently during my time at Webb House.

The first day flew and by the close I had completed the induction policies and procedures for the building and submitted the documentation for my staff ID. On my way home, I felt good. Good in a sense that I felt I was going to enjoy myself in my new role since the people were pleasant and even chatty. Yet, although I felt happy, I reserved judgement as past experiences taught me to be aware of people. So, I fixed and wore my resident default mask when settling into new environments – my *'non-committal mask'*. The one that portrayed a pleasant, professional but cautious nature, not getting too comfortable until I was satisfied and happy. It was a wise move on my part as I did not have long to wait for a certain individual's true colours to show.

Further Down the Road...

I survived for six whole months and so far, had no complaints and loved working there. The work was varied, and there were so many people around the same age as me which was quite refreshing. I even made a couple of friends too and to this day, we were still close. My time thus far was a great learning experience and I generally got on with everyone. Still, there was a niggling doubt at the back of my mind.

Through my enjoyment, I still had the ups and downs but life, generally, was good and I was enjoying my role, I even got a chance to work and gain insight and experience in the bank's library which held the books and journals for staff doing their banking exams. Talk about a cornucopia of knowledge and experience, I was feasting on this and loving it.

Out of the Heart the Mouth Speaks...

Although I worked for the administration manager, all secretarial staff, including the principal secretary, shared one office and she ran a tight ship, discouraging talking. As we were told, we were there to work and work we did and some days when I came into the room, only the sound of keys on keyboards could be heard tapping away.

On one particular occasion, reports were coming in from the Caribbean about devastating weather conditions there. The region was experiencing a hurricane. In the office, despite what was said about idle chit chat, conversation was in full flow led by the principal secretary herself as she held centre stage, talking excitedly about property, investments and work being done with new appliances and fittings. It sounded interesting and even exciting but conversations like this were rare. So, we milked that moment because we knew that once the topics were exhausted, it would be back to no talking and getting the work done. After the conversation had subsided, we started talking about other things, so I decided to share what was going on in my life and talked about my mother, now living in Jamaica. She would return to the UK every six months or so, visiting her siblings, children and grandchildren. She had also bought land, built her house, grew and sold fruits, vegetables and sugar cane; I guess you could say she was a fulltime farmer!

It was at this time - September 1988 - when Hurricane Gilbert raged across the Caribbean, heavily damaging Jamaica. My mother was in the process of building a house right next to my grandfather's home and had just finished working on it, when the hurricane hit. I shared how frightened I was whenever I spoke with her, listening firsthand to the angry storm, knowing the destruction it was leaving in its wake. My colleagues asked questions about whether there was electricity and the damage, especially to my mum's farm. I explained that my mother had solar panels fitted to the house which were attached to a large fuel generator and so she was okay. The conversation eventually petered out and I realised that while I had been sharing, the principal secretary never joined in, laughed at the funny bits or anything else; she just sat there, listening with an expressionless face. When I had finished, she asked, "How can your mother afford all of this?"

Her question came and was delivered, I felt, with the intention of making me self-conscious. It would not have had this effect had she acted as if she was interested in what I was saying; so, I was shaken. But then, it was not the question itself, really, but how it was asked, as if she disbelieved me. I felt affronted, enraged and disgusted. As far as I was concerned, her question came from a colonial mindset and before I replied, I stared at her as she sat there like I was a child and she, the mother, waiting for me to tell the truth. I spoke slowly, enunciating every word "My mother came to England when she was sixteen years old, to join her parents who had been here since the late 1950's; and she had worked very hard, saving her money so that she could buy her land and build herself a home, grow crops and live off the land when she retired."

I also informed her that my grandfather had worked extremely hard, saving every penny so that when he and my grandmother returned to Jamaica after spending twenty years in England, they could also happily retire. On reflection I was angry that she questioned where my mother had obtained her money from, treating me like I was telling one of Aesop's Fables, and that all I was saying was just a story; she made me feel as if Black people could not own land, build property or even have a good lifestyle. Yet, I really did not have to share this information with her as I wanted her to know that whatever thoughts or perceptions she had about Black people or more to the point about my family, she should immediately dispel them. Thereafter, I chose never to share any more personal information especially when she was in the office since there definitely was an indifference in her manner towards me. It was not long before her deep-seated feelings made another guest appearance.

Second Time Around...

In fact, it happened the following year and what transpired then really got me interested in understanding people and more importantly, their motives in the things they said and did. It really was a disagreement, but I was certain the principal secretary would have seen it as insubordination.

My family and I were going on a Canadian holiday to visit relatives on my mother's side. My sister, who was still a student nurse, had been given time off in June and the family decided to work around that month, booking our own annual leave dates. I happened to have mentioned it as I was talking to the other secretaries. The principal secretary overheard my dates and informed me that I could not have them since she and her husband always took vacation at that time. I was surprised, firstly because I was not actually talking to her and secondly, she was not my boss and had no power to sign off on my annual leave. I asked if she had booked her holiday yet. She said that it was unimportant whether she had booked or not, it was just that I was not allowed to have the dates I wanted. I was fuming, remembering our previous conversation the year before and thought she was now using any power and opportunity to hinder me. It felt as though she bore a grudge of some kind and was using her positon to belittle me. I made one last attempt to appeal to her better nature by letting her know that those dates were the best ones for my family, especially as my sister could not change hers. My words fell on deaf ears. She said I could not have the dates and made it clear that she neither cared nor was she interested in having any further discussions and, as far as she was concerned, it was over.

I was furious, yet knew she had no real power over whether I went or not, so I decided to speak to my boss. He knew nothing about the discussion between myself and the principal secretary, or the fact that she had denied my request. I ensured I saw him before she could, making sure to mention the principal secretary always had the same two weeks off each year. He smiled and said, "Of course Jacqui, we can't have you missing out on a family trip like that." I must have had the biggest grin ever as I thanked him, but my smugness was short-lived.

As a rule, all that went on in the office was reported back to the principal secretary and this included my holiday request being granted by my line manager. She had weekly meetings with all the directors and managers, discussing everything that happened, including the secretarial team. After her meeting and learning about my approach to my line manager, she was very curt with me. But I did not care, I did what I needed to do to make sure I would not miss out on my trip. A couple of weeks' after and another rare occasion, where we were all in an animated conversation, it turned to the subject of Christmas and what everyone was planning to do. Again, the principal secretary was at the centre, talking about what she and her family would be doing. I said nothing since I was unprepared to have another spat with her, but whether I wanted to interact with her or not, the hat-trick of our clashes came.

In the first four years working at the training centre I never got Christmas off and was part of the skeleton cover that was required of my position as a junior secretary, and as such my colleague and my responsibility. I was having a conversation with my friend - Kim Thompson - about not being allowed to have Christmas off and how boring it was to be in the centre since it would be virtually empty. Anyway, whilst the various conversations were going on, I asked the principal secretary if she always booked annual leave at Christmas.

She paused and gave me a long hard stare before replying through gritted teeth, "Look you got what you wanted." Nobody said anything and I was surprised at her ferocity. "All I wanted to do was sort this out calmly," she added. Of course, I was thinking about her denying me my request, leaving me no choice but to go higher up. I knew she was angry as she clearly felt she was being undermined. I responded, evenly, "Oh, is that what you were doing?"

I knew my reaction would provoke her even further and no sooner had the thought entered my mind, it came from her lips as she bellowed, "Do not be so facetious!"

I think even her own blast shocked her while the other secretaries stared on in disbelief. Still, I remained silent and though mad, controlled myself, managing not to retaliate as it would have only given her the opportunity to really have something against me. So, searching my desk drawer I found what I was looking for - an Oxford Dictionary. I had never heard the word 'facetious' before and needed to know what it meant. Upon finding it I read aloud, *"**Facetious:** to make an attempt at being funny, while being sarcastic at the same time."* After I read it, I made no reaction but returned it to my drawer and carried on working, without saying another word. She had lost. Right then I was really proud of myself, it was not worth any further aggravation, so I just left it there.

Years later, when I was expecting my daughter, I found out the reason as to why she had been so abrasive. Apparently, she had been going through a lot of personal problems and was not coping well. I guess, people coped in different ways with their personal problems and although I empathised at her predicament, I could not condone her behaviour towards me. Sometimes, people in positions of power took their own frustrations out on others and this bullying behaviour was used a lot in the workplace, especially when the bully had the power to take matters further. Yet, I learnt that people could only be made to feel small and insignificant, if they allowed others to treat them that way. Whether being talked down to or treated in an unkind manner and by handing over one's power, they were giving license for others to treat them as how they saw fit. This had been a big lesson and a steep learning curve for me. By understanding the concept and principles of emotional intelligence and by tapping into our emotions, we gain a better understanding of our emotional triggers and what heightens them but, we can also gain insight into other peoples' motives and emotions too. It was not worth fighting fire with fire, as in the end one could get consumed by the flames and to be honest, there were other ways and means to take the edge off how individuals have behaved towards you. In this respect, I used my own emotional intelligence to lay the foundation for my path to empowerment.

Chapter 5 - The Phoenix Rising from the Ashes

"She fell, she crashed, she broke she cried, she crawled, she hurt, she surrendered and then…she rose again."
~ Beautiful Minds Anonymous ~

After that dramatic outburst there were no further clashes between us as we both knew where we stood with each other. This gave us a platform where we were professional and courteous to each other like dancers, tiptoeing around and avoiding the other, getting on with things and doing what needed to be done. The chit chat sessions were now few and far between, like something had died and as a result of what had transpired all the joy was unceremoniously sucked from the room. It was obvious, true feelings and intentions were unfiltered and if the incidents were anything to go by, it meant that there was now an unwarranted target on my back. And to all intent and purposes, I felt like I had been transported right back into the planning department.

As part of my role, I would spend a day in the library, helping out, so I would always be on countdown whenever I was to be out of the office. I was grateful as those days gave me a little respite and even though it was quiet in the office, under the surface one could not help but feel that something was brewing; like a volcano waiting to erupt. So, I was glad that my time in the office was sparse, since it almost felt as if I needed to top up on my emotional resilience. The office environment suddenly felt devoid of emotion, interaction, joy or camaraderie; more like a desert without an oasis and this feeling only occurred whenever the principal secretary was around.

There was one particular training initiative that was underway. I liken it to an 'X Factor' style setup called The Potential Tutor's Programme. I was responsible for looking after the administration processes and really enjoyed it, understanding the concept since I had been looking after the programme for about a year. But I wanted more from it and yearned to be a participant, especially as I was a natural with technology and loved helping others. Not being involved was not an ideal situation for me and during lunchtime I would sit playing with the software, working out how to use it, then share with the other secretaries what I had learnt. I wanted to be a trainer and this programme was my ticket to becoming one.

When I think back it was funny. Instead of sending the secretaries on a course, a training video was sent in its place and, after watching this video, management expected the secretaries to miraculously hit the ground running, using it as if they were fully capable of doing so. Unfortunately for the department, this was definitely not the case, hence, my little training sessions and helpdesk support to others.

After a while, management got to hear of the sessions I was running and, I pondered on how I could best put myself forward as a potential participant. I really thought that with all my knowledge and experience, I would be approached by the director of the programme, but alas, I remained undiscovered. So, I decided if nobody was going to approach me, I needed to approach them and by taking the initiative with a bit of *'Dutch courage'*, I decided to go and see the director.

One day, I plucked up the courage after the completion of another successful workshop. I collected and collated the feedback forms and typed up the results. With all of this done, my sole intention was to ask him if he would consider me as a participant on the next programme. So, I did just that and asked him. He gave a long pause as I held my breath.

Then, he delivered something that knocked my self-esteem from one hundred to zero, saying... "Don't be silly Jacqueline, go and do the typing."

I was emotionally crushed.

Everything faded, my mind suddenly became blank as I walked out of his office, closing the door behind me. I could say I was calm, angry or even tearful, but I was none of these at the time, instead I was numb. I could have slammed his office door but I did not, I just kept thinking I was not as good as I thought I was. When I returned to my desk, I realised I still had the feedback responses in my hand, so I placed them on my desk and promptly left the office before anyone could see the tears in my eyes. I went to the sixth floor, where I knew the canteen and toilets would be empty (all the canteen staff and cleaners had left for the day). And just as I entered the toilet, my waterworks erupted, the salty torrents freely flowing. Anyone who happened to have entered those toilets, at that precise moment, would have found me in a real state and probably thought I had just heard some devastating news. I cried for what seemed like a lifetime before I finally stopped. Looking at myself in the mirror, I realised I looked awful and using cold water, I washed my face to remove the redness in my eyes and the flush on my skin. After a while, I managed to compose myself and returned to my office.

The principal secretary asked me where I had been since it seemed I may have been gone for a considerable amount of time. I just told her I had some stuff to do. I was unsure if it was the tone in my voice or the fact that she knew what had happened why she never said another word. As I settled at my desk I glanced to where I had left the feedback response sheets, but they were gone. I asked Kim, who sat opposite me, if she had picked them up. She said no, she had not. That was when the principal secretary told me that the director had asked her for them, so she had handed them over. There was a slight smirk on her face, and I knew then that the director had told her what had transpired while I was upstairs.

When I left for the day, Kim and I walked out of the office together; I told her what had happened. She was really empathetic and told me not to worry, because something would turn up and be just right for me. She was a lovely friend and, eventually, we became really close. Once, because I was under pressure with work and overlooked updating my To-Do-List, I had forgotten to print a document for one of the managers and received a rather harsh tongue-lashing from the principal secretary. I was beginning to realise that our working relationship was totally fractured and found it hard to get on with her.

One day, when no one was around in the office, Kim and I talked about the things which had been happening during my time there and what she had witnessed. Suddenly, she began to cry, saying it was not right what they were doing to me. She told me that the principal secretary was consistently informing senior managers about what was happening with me, as if she was building a case against me. There was one occasion when Kim overheard the principal secretary speaking to one of the directors about me, I supposed she felt Kim would not say anything and felt comfortable talking in front of her.

At one of the weekly meetings, my name came up. The managers asked the principal secretary what she thought of my abilities and of my request to be considered as a participant on the programme. I already knew she made it look like I was trying go above my station and the attitude towards me and a comment by my boss, alerted me to this fact. Whatever she told them, they were not going to entertain any further requests or discussions from me. I was destroyed when I learnt this but at least I knew why they had this attitude towards me. She had finally exacted her revenge. The right opportunity had presented itself and she had grabbed it and won It seemed that she was going to ensure that any career aspirations I had as a trainer, were going to be squashed before they had even begun. I was totally deflated and defeated.

The Fallout

After this incident life pretty much continued but I had lost my zeal and spark for the role. Sure, aside of doing my day-to-day tasks, I still supported others to understand the software or answered queries, I no longer felt the enthusiasm I once had. This went on for months and although I tried shrugging it off, something had changed. It was torture for me knowing I was doing all of this to enhance and promote the programme but was unable to even take part in it. It felt like I was getting all the ingredients to bake a fabulous cake and unable to eat it.

Since my knock down from the director, the principal secretary was chatting more than ever, even asking me questions every chance she got which were sometimes quite insignificant. It felt as if she relished in my failure. But I took it in my stride because I knew that she was just waiting for another opportunity to really drive home her wedge, punishing me in some other way. So, I made sure everything I did was on point, leaving little or no room for her to exert her authority over me again. Throughout the building, though, word spread about what had happened to me, especially since the principal secretary was friendly with a couple of the tutors.

All of the trainers in the training centre were white, except for one Indian woman while I was one of three Black women, all of us were in administrative roles. Knowing that a Black secretary fancied herself as a trainer was totally unheard of so, when any of her tutor friends came into the office, they greeted me; with that knowledge. You see, prior to the incident, none of them made any effort to talk to me or any of the other secretaries. Then, all of a sudden, they were making the effort. Coincidence? I did not think so. It bothered me just the same because I knew in my heart, I could do what they did - if given the opportunity. I never let on to the disappointment I felt, and got really good at wearing my mask, safeguarding me and my emotions.

Although I enjoyed working at the training centre, the incident got me thinking about changing my environment and I began looking for internal jobs. As part of the application process, an applicant's manager needed to be informed by Human Resources that the individual was applying for a job and would ask the manager whether they were satisfied for the application to proceed. That was insane, it meant that if a manager did not want you to progress, they could block your application, ultimately leaving the individual with no alternative but to resign. Even so, I was not ready to leave and decided to ride out this particular storm, knowing that sooner or later, the right role would come up.

The Winds of Change

The winds of change were blowing, and a way was about to open for me. I knew all too well that patience was truly a virtue and when one had the ambition to swiftly progress towards goals and aspirations, there was no choice but to be resilient, learn new things and equip oneself for what was to finally come. I did.

One day while doing tasks for the next training programme, I happened to bump into the department's audio-visual technician. He would film the participants, capturing their progress and their feedback sessions with the trainer. He asked how I was getting on and apologised in the same breath since he said he had heard about what had happened and the rebuff I received from the director. There were no secrets in the training centre. I shrugged, saying there was no need for him to apologise as these things happened. He then asked if I had ever done desktop publishing before. I said I had not. He asked if I wished to learn. I said yes. As the AV technician, he filmed the bank's adverts for television and so on and when people talked about him and the work he did, they spoke with reverence I could not quite understand until I got the chance to be taught by him. He seemed genuinely pleased that I had accepted his offer.

There was a little spring in my step as I returned to the office, this was my first ray of sunshine. I never mentioned a thing to anyone since I did not want anything or anyone spoiling my chance. The next day I made my way to his studio during my lunch break and was in awe when I arrived. I felt very privileged since he disliked anyone in his space, unless they were invited. That first day we just talked and he showed me the equipment and software I would be trained on. We then came to an agreement on when I would attend and how many times a week it would be. When I left his studio I was floating. I was being taught something other secretaries were not. I was elated at being asked and somewhere in the back of my mind I wondered why he was doing this.

We met three times a week, during my lunch break which suited me just fine and I still said nothing to my colleagues. This went on for three months. By then the AV technician would leave his studio door on the latch for me, allowing me to close it whenever my time was up. He had also set me assignments ranging from creating documents to booklets. Finally, my three months were up, and the AV technician said it had been his pleasure and if I ever needed to top-up my skills, to just let him know. He also said that with my new knowledge I could start looking for a new job. He had been correct as I needed to move on with my career, so I started looking for internal jobs, still not letting my colleagues know what I had been doing or the new skills I had acquired.

It did not take long, before a role came up in Moorgate, in the same building where I had my interview and typing test - a definite blast from the past! Since then, there had been many significant milestones I had reached along the way, the most important one being my decision to move to London and leaving my family behind. I had taken those definitive steps to branch out on my own; now, my journey had certainly taken me full circle.

I was unable to drive, though, and it meant taking the tube again, working in a different department and location. The department was a fairly new and I was both excited and apprehensive when I completed the application and mailed it, hoping and praying I would be shortlisted. At this point, I did not care if my line manager or the principal secretary were contacted, requesting a reference as I had nothing to lose and everything to gain. I must say I was on tender hooks as I waited for an acknowledgement or an interview invitation. Anything. It was three weeks later that I received a letter inviting me to an interview and I was ecstatic. I thought I would pop, my face cracking into a big cheesy grin while I walked around the office. Even when a colleague passed a comment about me looking a lot happier than I had been for a long while, I just responded, "Yes I am."

When the interview day arrived, I took half-day annual leave, drove into work and parked; arriving early and hoping I would not bump into anyone I knew. I even packed a change of clothes so that nobody knew where I had been. It was quite an elaborate plan, a bit like Mission Impossible but to me it was *Mission Possible*. As I sat in the lobby outside where the interviews were taking place, I looked around and saw a shelf with a range of software packages in their cellophane wrapping - the same packages I had been taught by the AV technician!

I was greeted by a tall Black woman who then led me into the interview. I knew I had made an impression once they began talking about starting dates. Then, they asked if I had any questions for them. I said I had noticed the software packages and wondered if these were the ones being used by the secretary. They said they had been sitting on shelf for a while and would be delighted if whoever got the job could use them, otherwise that would be a waste. I lost no time in explaining I had been trained on all the packages. A couple of days later I found I had been successful. When the principal secretary heard, she congratulated me with a lovely smile which made me slightly nervous but that feeling passed, since I was thrilled. I was even more surprised when I was congratulated by my other colleagues. I felt like a celebrity. There was no fanfare though and before long I was starting my new job.

A new chapter had begun and the lessons I had learnt to temper my emotions and not raise to an individuals' tactics of keeping me oppressed were of great benefit. Although they were harsh lessons, they helped shaped who I was to become and more importantly, how I developed and grew.

During my time at the training centre with all the good experiences, came the disappointing ones too. I could not control how others perceived me, how I was treated or even what was said to me. What I could only govern were my emotions, especially in how I responded. The first lesson I learnt was forgiveness, it was hard at first but became easier when I understood the issues from the other persons' perspective. Sometimes, I needed to walk in someone else's shoes to really understand where they were coming from and what they were going through. I also learnt not to relinquish my own personal power or authority to another person; irrespective of how senior they were to me. Through this experience, I learnt my most valuable lesson, to have more confidence in myself and my abilities and, more importantly, to continue pursuing my goals and aspirations regardless of the landscape and terrain I was navigating. Determination, strength of character and a great support network and a 'Sistahood' of friends and family were also essential in my empowerment.

Chapter 6 - Confidence Leads to Competence

"...by stretching yourself beyond your perceived level of confidence you accelerate your development of competence."
~ Michael J. Gelb ~

The Journey So Far...

I have shared with you my personal experiences of being bullied. In this particular chapter, I share not only my observations but, importantly, my first-hand knowledge of the systematic bullying and harassment of one particular member of staff, who actually worked in another department. In her desperation, she sought the support of two managers in our team and a safe haven within our office. Do not get me wrong, I had my fair share of personal incidents within this department during the time I worked there; especially when certain managers tried to leave some kind of mark. I endured these *'slings and arrows'* with dignity and grace, triumphantly overcoming their prejudices, biases and negative working practices.

A New and Different Direction

Well, the day finally arrived, I was starting a new role. I was warmly welcomed by Bert, a white senior manager. He introduced me to the rest of the team, most of who were white bar Lola, the one Black female manager. I settled quickly and although the work was different, it was very interesting. I even managed to find some 'me' time, opening the software packages I previously saw. A few days into my new role, I was informed that a junior secretary would be joining us, doing the bulk of the administrative duties and general typing. It was just as well because the kind of work being churned out by the managers was of a very high volume and I alone was unable to cope with it.

In the late 1980's there were certain working practices including new buzzwords going around. During this time there was a lot of talk about creating the banks' *competency framework*, not just within our own organisation but across the entire Square Mile (a term used for all businesses situated within the City of London's square mile). Organisations were also bringing onboard external consultants to create their frameworks, often linked to appraisal systems and other personal development processes.

Our office was a hive of activity with consultants coming and going, a few days a week. When they were present, we produced copious amounts of neatly typed transcripts from their handwritten notes and on some days when I left the office to go home, it would be the first time I actually exhaled. That was how the work came thick and fast.

Six months after joining, the bank had their annual intake of graduates. There were two streams - the general graduates and the *cream of the crop* graduates, who were on a six month fast-track programme to get them into a management role. Three males and three females were on this fast-track programme and one of them was a lovely young Black woman named Sarah. She was really friendly, always smiling whenever she came into our office. Our senior manager, Bert and Lola, were the only ones who made her feel welcome and so, Sarah naturally gravitated towards them. They took an interest in her development and were always helpful, sharing their knowledge and making time for her if she had any queries. But while all the graduates were achieving their milestones quite effortlessly Sarah was not, and after one month, I noticed she was in our office more often than usual; she would go directly to Bert and Lola either into a meeting room or by their desks, and speak with them.

One day Sarah came into the office and seemed down and not her cheerful, smiling self. She looked stressed as if she had been crying. Bert, Lola and Sarah were by my desk when she suddenly blurted out that she was very harassed and that her director, who was supposed to be mentoring her, hardly paid her any attention, let alone help her to develop her skills. She said she was not being treated or supported in the same way as her five white counterparts and described the things they had done and the meetings they had attended as part of *their* development. We were in an open plan office and everybody heard. When she was finished, there was silence, nobody spoke, after a while Bert said, "Well, you know he's racist!"

I could not believe what I had just heard from a senior manager. It was already upsetting for Sarah and I was angry since what he had said was to someone who was clearly distressed. Later, those very same words returned to haunt him. Sarah burst into tears and was quickly ushered into another room. I took the initiative and made tea for the three of them. When I entered, I noticed she had stopped crying but was repeating over and over that she could not understand why this director hated her. I felt sorry for her and really wanted to give her a hug but, instead, excused myself to return with a box of tissues. Both managers thanked me on my return. And as I remember looking and thinking about this very talented yet broken young Black woman who was being mistreated. I sincerely believed she was being discriminated against since she had not been given the same opportunities or treated equally.

The Darkness Before the Dawning

I did not see Sarah much after that, and often wondered what had happened to her after her meltdown. I was unsure if she was embarrassed but knew that if it had been me, I would never return want to work again. It was a couple of months later before I heard anything more about Sarah and this was by chance.

It was a Friday and I had planned a weekend away from London. Whilst organising my work calendar for the following week I happened to overhear a conversation between the managers. Since I was located at the other end of the office, the managers probably felt I could not hear but I listened as I completed my work. By now, word had gotten to Sarah's supposed mentor that she had an emotional meltdown. It amazed me, when I heard what Human Resources were going to do as a result of him contacting them, saying he no longer wished to mentor her. Somehow, he made it look like Sarah was not very good with her tasks and suggested that they moved her to another location and a new mentor. When Sarah finally heard what her director, with the backing of HR, were going to do about her development she became even more distressed and so distraught that she went to her doctor who signed her off sick, citing workplace stress as the reason.

I was angry, even though I did not know her very well, I felt her pain and the injustice meted out to her. But as a junior secretary, I could not comment or say anything and instead spoke with Lola, whom Sarah had kept in contact with. That opportunity came a couple of weeks later. In confidence I told her what I had overhead, sharing my thoughts about Sarah's treatment. Being the only two Black women in the department, having a conversation with each other was a source of comfort and as we talked, I learnt about what Sarah was going through and at how devastated she was with her lack of progress and the director cutting her loose. All of this had been delivered to her by a letter from HR and not the director. This only added to her stress. What made it worse, her peers had been assigned their first junior management roles. I could only imagine how she felt as the director had systematically destroyed her career prospects by denying her any form of development. A young Black, and extremely talented graduate, had been relegated to a much lesser role than her peers and that was so unfair and wrong.

I later found out that she had been assigned a role outside of London, roughly ten miles from where she lived in Hertfordshire, and it seemed that even though she was still being given an opportunity to be mentored and prepared for a management role, she would have to do so outside of London. This move ultimately affected her London Weighting - *London Weighting* was a basic salary addition for living in London due to the city's living expenses – and she saw a massive reduction in how much he previously received.

It was only a matter of time before her stress levels consumed her and she became very ill. It seemed that even Sarah's new relocated role was not giving her the experience or the career leverage she had hoped for. And to add insult to injury, the "new" manager turned out to be a close friend of the director who had disparaged her. I was certain this too increased her anxiety levels, sinking her deeper into her illness. On another occasion, Lola shared that Sarah was moving departments and manager, and this time it was on her request. On her return from three-months sick leave, she immediately spoke to HR, requesting an immediate transfer. She had said that she was so sick and traumatised by what the manager had said as soon as she joined that she had decided it was not worth subjecting herself to any further victimisation, bullying or harassment. So, HR reassigned her to a department a lot closer to her home.

She settled quite well, and slowly began to regain her confidence with the support of her new manager, who assigned her work she was more than capable of doing. I was pleased to hear this since she was at last coming out of the darkness that hung over her for such a long time. It had been two years since she walked through our office door, introducing herself as a new fast-track graduate, and that shocked me. I was deeply saddened to know that this was not a one-off situation and this soul-destroying situation had not only affected her.

This type of behaviour happened (and was still happening) to many people in all walks of life, jobs and industries, and her story could resonate with those who have been or were in the same position. Unfortunately, this treatment was endemic. It has been going on for a long time with a template being avidly used by those in positions of power, to block or stifle the career opportunities of talented Black and minority ethnic men and women. As a result, these brilliant people suffered illness, stress and other mental health related issues which have impacted their lives inside and outside of the workplace.

A Light at the End of the Tunnel

One day, Lola and I arranged to meet for lunch outside of work. Since an office move was taking place, this allowed us plenty of time to be out without anyone noticing. I was glad to hear that Sarah's health was improving and she had started court proceedings against the organisation and director, plus, anyone else directly or indirectly involved with her deplorable treatment. She knew she had been victimised and discriminated against, both of which were massively contrary to the organisation's development and career progression policy. Sarah was going all out when it came to her being compensated since she knew what she was due and where she would have been in career, had she finished the programme.

Sarah had regained her confidence and had a supportive network of people who, on learning of her ill-treatment, encouraged her to take her case further. She was feeling much better and ready to take them to an employment tribunal to get justice. Using her professionalism and expertise she organised the evidence of various documents, and was in essence, using her skills against them. This was where Bert's words returned to haunt him as Sarah was able to recall – verbatim - the conversation she had when things had started to go downhill and when she had sought solace in our office. It also was not difficult to see the effect Sarah's claim had on Bert and ever since the issues came to light, there was a noticeable change in him. He no longer laughed or joked with us and his interactions became more formal. I kind of felt sorry that he had been drawn into it but what he had said was heard by all who were present and even if he tried denying it, other people could be drawn into the matter too.

A court date was set and as it drew closer Bert seemed to shrink, it was as if he had suddenly lost his authority. I knew he was worried and all I thought of was the saying 'loose lips, sink ships'. I was certain that if what he had said was disclosed in court, his career would be over; no further progression or even his resignation. While I mourned the loss of her career and what hardship there may have been for Sarah, I rejoiced in the victory that had been gained through her resilience. And at the eleventh hour, Sarah was approached by the bank with a compensation package for her loss of career, earnings and the stress she had endured. It was substantial and I was so happy for her when I found out. As much as I was excited for her, I thought about the bank's lost opportunity with someone whom they originally earmarked as one of their leaders of the future.

Although this happened many years ago, I still feel the emotions around it but most of all, how Sarah's story resonated with me and my own Journey to Empowerment. There were so many valuable lessons I learnt from this experience. I took to heart Sarah's great courage and confidence to do what she needed to do; knowing there would be opposition, bullying, harassment and many obstacles blocking her path. I admired the resilience she showed in the face of adversity and her strength of character in doing what was right even though she was alone. I learnt that one needed to stand by one's values and principles and, more importantly, not to allow others to discourage you from your goals and aspirations. I learnt that I could be more than a conqueror, if I continued to be my authentic self, and to me, this meant never relinquishing my authority, my power or being afraid in challenging the status quo. Being a proud and professional Black woman, I am grounded in who I am, never giving up my ethnicity or the essence of my character, in order to 'fit in' anywhere.

Chapter 7 - As One Door Closed…

*"As one door closes, another opens;
but we often look so long and so
regretfully upon the closed door that
we do not see the one which has opened for us."*
~ Alexander Graham Bell ~

Where My Training Began

By the time Sarah's case ended the entire department had settled back at Webb House. It had been a few years since I had left, and things were now very different. We reverted to the very floor I worked on before and where new departments now occupied the space. I wandered around the building, speaking to the people I knew who still worked there. There was no principal, directors, team of secretaries and the main administration office – were all gone. The library, though, was still there and I was pleased to find that the librarian was too. It was lovely seeing her again. We talked about the good old days and she filled me in on what had happened since I had left. It was nice catching up. I felt like the *'Prodigal's Daughter'*, returning home after a very long time out in the world.

I headed to the principal's office and was immediately taken aback. I had forgotten how lovely and lush the carpet was as my feet sunk into it. Even the AV technician's studio was gone, his studio now used to store surplus office equipment. Training had also changed and although the trainers were still based there, a lot of the training was done offsite. Even the much hailed, X-Factor style tutor-training programme was no longer offered; dissolving when the management had replaced it with a train-the-trainer programme and the chance to study for a Certificate in Training Practice (CTP), run by the Chartered Institute of Personnel Development (CIPD).

Opportunity Knocked on My Door

Everything pretty much flowed well for quite a while, but things were about to change again. The banks' competency framework was nearing completion, so I knew something was wrong when Bert asked if there was any personal development training that I was interested in undertaking. I took a short time to think about it, since all I ever wanted to be was a trainer and here I was, years later, being asked if I wanted to develop myself. I wasted no time and said I wished to do the CTP, on a six-month fast-track programme. Bert agreed and because things were slow in the department, asked if I wanted to go part-time with the very tutors who would be training me on the programme. I was elated and accepted and a month later, I started part-time. By the time the month was up, work around the framework had all but dried up. My part-time role was a definite blessing. In fact, a double blessing since I was able to work with Franklin, the manager of the training department. I later found out that in his youth, he was in the British Army, retiring at the rank of major and secretly, we called him the "Sergeant Major". When I had joined the team, he asked me if I would like to support him while I studied for the certificate. I was also curious about his work since his team were self-sufficient and autonomous, all their workshops and training already scheduled for the entire year.

He told me that he was also co-authoring a book on training and needed someone to edit and type up the transcripts. He said I would be in a prime position as I would be reading the book before it was even published. I laughed and thought, yes, I *would* be in a good position. So, I took up his offer, agreeing to type his book on some days and train on the other days. Things worked out very well for me. Soon, I was introduced to Franklin's friend and co-author over the phone since he did not live in London; because of this, we needed to courier his submitted documents to and fro.

My typing speed and the accuracy were just as good as when I was doing it fulltime; I was and still am, eternally grateful to my mother for sending me on that typing course when I was younger. Soon, the co-author and I eventually established a good working relationship. He was easy to talk to and would even crack a joke or two; I was quite comfortable typing his submissions or contacting him if I had any queries or misunderstood what he had sent. At the same time, I was still studying whilst working with some of the tutors as part of my assessment. It was a really strange setup but it worked. The very programme I had coveted when I worked as a copy typist all those years ago, was being delivered as part of the CTP programme. This tickled me even more as I thought about when the director rejected me, only to be given a lifeline by the AV technician. I smiled and thought if I ever saw that director again, I would shake his hand and thank him. Here I was, moving forwards, acquiring new skills and developing other competencies which would place me into a more senior job. I had indeed come full circle and was so glad and grateful to have been given the opportunity to not only undertake the programme but work as a junior trainer as well.

As time went on the book began to take shape and so had my progress on the programme. As it neared its completion, I spent more time helping with the book. Before long, though, I was submitting my whole portfolio for a final assessment; gaining my certificate and the long-awaited title of Qualified Trainer. Finally, the book was also completed, published and ready for purchase. It had been such an exciting and momentous journey for me since I had been there from the beginning and at the end, and still yet to meet the co-author. So, a book launch was organised and we were told that he was coming to celebrate with the entire team in London. The author and I were going to meet, face-to-face, finally.

The day arrived and a restaurant was booked. My manager and the rest of the team eagerly awaited the co-author's arrival. When it was announced that he had finally arrived; my manager went down to reception to collect him. As my manager stepped from the lift with the co-author, he walked to where I stood and said, "I first have to introduce you to Jacqui, the woman who helped us make this happen." The look on the co-author's face was priceless, it was if he had actually vocalised: *"You're Black!"*

I shook his hand, smiled and said it was a pleasure to put a face to the name. He smiled, but I saw he was finding it hard to stay composed. I was unsure as to what he was expecting and only assumed that he thought the team was like him - white. I felt embarrassed for him since we had developed a rapport over the phone, laughing and talking about anything and everything. It was not just about the pleasantries or the book either, he would normally enquire whether I had a good weekend or, how I was in general and I would ask him about himself or about other things he may have told me.

We made our way to the restaurant, I felt there was an uncomfortable air at our table as if everyone knew that the co-author seemed different, somehow. The actual conversations with him seemed wooden and awkward. He was also a bit reserved, and not as friendly as he had been before over the phone. It was a real shame how things turned out. We limped through lunch then returned to the office, the whole celebration had gone damp, as if a cloud was hanging over the conversations, even the laughter sounded more nervous than jovial.

I did have my suspicions that it was because I was Black; and recalled a conversation I once had with a person whom I had never met but had a lot of dealings with over the phone. When we finally met, they would say, "It's nice to put a face to the name." but, "You don't sound Black on the phone." To which I had responded, "What does Black sound like?" They were unable to answer.

After the book launch, the co-author was never the same with me over the phone again. If he needed to speak to my manager, he would always be polite, never encouraging any form of conversation like our previous conversations and this was such a shame as we had a good working relationship. Now that I had completed my studies and was a qualified trainer and the book launch had taken place, it was time for me to return to my department on a fulltime basis. I had no leaving do but was presented with a lovely gift and card and a signed copy of the book which I treasure and still have today. After all, I helped to create it and even though six or seven revisions have been made since, I lay claim to the fact that I typed the original one.

A Time to Transition

Upon my return to my department things felt a little strange. There had been rumours of imminent changes and that redundancies were about to happen. I had not paid much attention to what was being said and no one knew if there was any truth to the rumours circulating. It was like Chinese Whispers, so I thought it best to wait and see. I did not have long to wait – in fact, soon after returning to the department, everyone received a memo informing us that the senior director of Learning Networks was coming to have meetings with all the departments. Apparently, this was to allay any fears the staff had about the redundancy rumours. I reserved my judgement, keeping my thoughts to myself, awaiting the official meeting. Plus, I was not alarmed at the thought of being made redundant, only curious about what the process would be. The meeting day finally arrived, and I had never seen Bert so nervous as we filed into a meeting room where the Head was waiting. He introduced himself and said why he was here with us. He went on to explain the memo and the consulting company who had been brought in to evaluate the downsizing exercise. As the director talked, I intently listened, watching his body language. I could see that he was uneasy at delivering the news.

Finally, he got to the end of his presentation. Of course, Bert and a couple of the other managers asked some questions and although they were intelligent, they did not relate to the reason why we were at the meeting; as if they were just showing that they were on top of everything. For me, there was only one question I needed to ask and after watching the director; the more he spoke, the more I saw. It was as if his mouth was saying one thing but his eyes told a different story. So, I plucked up the courage to ask, "What's the bank going to do with the data once they received it from the external consultancy firm?" There was a long pause and I felt the managers' eyes on me. I was sure a couple of the mouths that were slightly agape, along with the director, had not expected anyone to ask about the data once it was with this external American company. I smiled as I waited for a reply. I had unsettled him with my question and, as he started his response, I listened. He said that the organisation would keep the data for their own use since it was just an exercise they wanted to conduct, to see where the organisation currently was at. Now, it did not take a genius to realise that what had been given as an answer was not in fact an answer but still, I accepted his response. Nodding and smiling, knowing full well that he had just sidestepped the question with a blatant lie. He knew full well what the organisation would do and me asking a question would not change a thing.

After the meeting, Lola asked me why I had asked the question, I said that what the director had told us made no sense and that I felt a cull was about to take place across the whole learning network. She said that was not going to happen and that I was mistaken. I thought to myself, we'll see, you'll be coming back to me, asking how I knew. Well, a few weeks after our meeting and the subsequent ending of the consultation, we all received 'the' memo. It was a Friday afternoon. We were called into another meeting where Bert delivered the news. The message was clear, succinct and to the point, redundancies were going to occur across the entire Learning Network throughout the UK. I knew something would happen but never envisaged it would be a mass cull. After the meeting Lola came to me and asked how I knew and jokingly called me a "witch". You see, I previously had made a few personal predictions that had actually come true; they were funny but in this case, it was a serious situation.

The news was a shock to everyone else and although we had an idea something was coming, we had no idea of the magnitude. Shortly after, late one afternoon, the news was delivered. Bert said he would like to talk with me and booked a meeting room for himself, Angela - my line manager – and myself. Since I rarely was in the office, Angela was not in the picture much during the time I spent studying and working in the training department, so there was little interaction between us. So, I listened as they both spoke. Basically, I was told that I was being put on the 'at risk of redundancy' register and needed to start looking for alternative roles. If a suitable one was not found, then redundancy would be considered. I was given a sheet with the internal vacancies to look at and during our conversation they outlined my options. I thought I had no chance of redundancy because there were plenty of internal jobs available that I could easily get, only if I stayed as a secretary. But since I had now passed my qualifications and was a qualified trainer, the role of a secretary was not an option for me to consider, even if that was what they were really inferring for me to apply for.

I quickly realised that they were not concerned about me moving into a role where I could use my newly acquired skills and qualifications. All the same I did not push the issue since it was not an option I could explore. So, I went through the process, looking and applying for the roles I could do. Then one day, Angela came to me asking if everything was okay. I responded that I had just looked at the job sheet and there was nothing matching my skillset and qualifications. She said that if no suitable internal jobs were available, they would give me time off to look for an external one. I was fuming but thanked her without further comment. Sensing a change in my mood she tried being friendly, probing for a reaction. I said I had nothing more to say and would keep looking for internal roles. Whether she believed me or not I did not care. After thirteen years in the bank I was not about to walk away without nothing and if I was going to leave, it was going to be with my redundancy package. So, that following weekend, I thought long and hard about how I would do that.

The Coin Has Two Faces

The following Monday morning, I went into the office and it felt strange for many reasons. I was no longer seen as working there and it felt as if I had already left the department and organisation. The atmosphere was a real dog-eat-dog one, where everyone sought to secure their own job and since I was the most junior, my position was at risk. Plus, with my line manager suggesting I looked for jobs outside of the bank, I realised they did not want me to have the redundancy package; so, I kept quiet about what I was doing. The truth of the matter was, my senior manager would need to make the redundancy payment out of the department's budget, and I guess he did not want to deplete it by paying a lump sum to lowly me.

Eventually, I became quite annoyed at the fact that Angela seemed to be always there, in my face, asking me how I was and, more to the point, what I was doing. It was as if she was keeping close tabs on me. I knew it was her role as my line manager but the frequency in which she had done this, was bordering on harassment. So, I remained closed to her and the other managers, not disclosing too much but giving updates in line with the redundancy process. At last, the twelve-week period and criteria to find a suitable role had expired, and I had all the evidence I needed to show I had been applying for jobs with the actual outcomes. I passed this onto both Bert and Angela and was soon called into another meeting with them. I expected them to say I had exhausted the process and would now be placed on the redundancy list. Not so. In fact, Bert suggested I took an extra twelve weeks to further look for jobs. Angela agreed with him, even suggesting I look for other roles lesser than what I could do as a way of staying within the organisation. I have no idea why they thought that was a suitable option, I said nothing. When I did speak, I referred them to the redundancy process and guidelines, and that it had been twelve weeks, the timescale given for this process to conclude. I also pointed out that there was nothing in the policy or procedures that alluded to it being changed at the manager's discretion. I further emphasised that if I was forced to do so it could be deemed as constructive dismissal since I would have been forced to resign as no suitable internal jobs were available. I was angry at their bare-faced suggestions. On hearing my reference to constructive dismissal Bert became very unprofessional, flippant and threatening in the tone and inflection of his voice. "Yes, you could go down the constructive dismissal route but trust me, you wouldn't get the same payout as in a redundancy package."

I was not surprised by his reaction, since he was the same manager who a couple of years previously, had made *'that comment'* to Sarah. I simply responded saying, if I was forced to leave I would then go down the constructive dismissal route since it would be as a result of an injustice being meted out to me. Bert looked like he was ready to explode as he struggled to keep his composure. He then said we needed to discuss the matter further but at another time and at which point, he stood, promptly leaving the room. Poor Angela, she looked so embarrassed after Bert left and I asked if there was anything she would like to add to what had been said, she shook her head and said there was nothing. So, we both left the meeting room.

Nothing more was said that day, the next or for one entire week. I knew that what I had said had messed up their plans but I did not care, I was not going to be brushed off because someone felt I should stay and accept a lesser role or if I was going to leave; they rather I forfeited my redundancy package. I later heard how Bert was livid and had rung his boss ranting about how I had mentioned constructive dismissal in the meeting. It probably was like tempting a bull with a red flag but he must have thought I had *'welcome wipe your feet here'*, embossed on my forehead, failing to realise that I had read every bit of paper pertaining to the redundancy process; so I knew what I was up against. Angela eventually told me that they would put me forward for redundancy, since I had in effect satisfied the criteria. I already had known that I had met the criteria, but I think they had really underestimated my determination. They knew I was determined and strove to achieve my goals but, I think this situation, made them realise that if they had persisted on me doing another twelve-week job search, I would have taken it further up the managerial chain.

So, here I was, being made redundant for the first time in my life but I was extremely happy about leaving. When I first joined the bank in my early twenties, I was told that a job in a bank was for life but, for me, I wanted more than what the banking environment was offering me as a Black woman and a professional. I was uncertain of where I wanted to go, but I had always fancied gaining experience working in merchant banks like Lehman Brothers or Deutsche Bank. So, I applied to some of them when I was first looking externally at roles in the merchant banking arena; and even though I met all the job requirements, I was still being rejected. This puzzled me, until one day while talking to a friend, an ex-bank clerk; I learnt that because I had worked in a clearing bank, merchant banks would not touch me with a 'cocktail stick'. I had not realised there was this type of snobbery in the banking arena. Well, I think it was absolutely true since I had written letters, sent out my CV or applied for roles through recruitment agencies, always being turned down! To be quite frank, after spending thirteen years in the same organisation, I really wanted to see what it was like in others. So, I decided to go temping rather than look for permanent roles. I was not really fussed as to what industry, but rathered another large legal or financial services organisation.

The Last Mile Was the Longest

It was not long before all the required paperwork for my redundancy arrived, it felt so strange. I had a feeling of acceptance that things were finally happening, and in a way, it was almost like old times. Conversations in the office were better and questions about what I was going to do were asked but I never said much. My focus had shifted to my leaving do. I wanted this to be a momentous and memorable occasion because after all, I most definitely deserved it! I wanted to have something *different* as a parting of a 13-year long union. You see, leaving do's back then consisted of boxes of white and red wine, soft drinks and plenty of nibbles but that was not my style. So, I approached Bert and told him I would like to organise my own leaving event. He was taken aback as it was not 'the done thing' and it would have been up to Angela and the other team members to arrange my leaving do event. He agreed just the same. I also told him that it would be an invitation only leaving do. Again, he agreed. I was looking to celebrate with the people who I wanted to be there since, the norm there was any leaving do would include everyone - whether known to the person or not.

I decided to have a Caribbean-themed leaving do and spoke to a very talented Black woman - who happened to be the head chef at the training centre - I asked her where she could undertake the cooking of West Indian food for my leaving do. The sumptuous buffet would consist of curried goat or mutton, rice and peas, coleslaw and salad with plantain, Jamaican patties and other delights; washed down with tropical, non-alcoholic punch. What a feast! I also decided to add a few bottles of wine, for those that fancied a tipple. My event was going to be completely authentic, with tropical looking artificial plants and tropical pictures on the wall for affect and, not forgetting the smooth sounds of reggae music playing in the background, creating the ultimate Caribbean vibe. The Principal's office was the perfect venue and better yet, it was located at the end of a corridor where nobody worked, so my event would disturb no-one.

News travelled fast and word soon got around that I was being made redundant - one day, two women were overheard talking by Marj a close friend of mine.

Woman One: *"Are you going to Jacqui's leaving do?"*

Woman Two: *"I'm not sure, if I'm not busy I'll pop along."*

Marj asked them if they were invited, to which they both said: *"What!?"*

"Yes, it's invitation only." Marj responded. Later, when she told me, she said the looks on their faces was priceless.

Soon, my last day arrived and, I was in for a big surprise. The department had also planned something which I knew absolutely nothing about, catching me totally off guard. A table had been booked at Simpsons-in-the Strand, where we all had breakfast. This went down well and upon returning to the office I went to see the head chef, as I needed to ensure that everything was set and ready for my own event. When it happened, I had the time of my life. My thirteen-year celebration was wrapped up in one pleasant afternoon. I told my colleagues a heartfelt farewell and left with very few regrets.

I knew I was moving towards something better, and felt things were changing for me, even after the experiences of indifference, racism and bullying. I walked away acknowledging that I had overcome those negative experiences. I embraced my confidence like a close friend, knowing that the next chapter of my life was opening up and that I would be approaching it with a different attitude and mindset.

Chapter 8 - A Temporary Solution

"To find yourself, think for yourself."
~ Socrates ~

I opened my eyes on Monday morning, had a good stretch and switched on the TV - then it dawned on me - I was still in bed! I was ready to rush to the bathroom since I hated being late for work but, slowly, the events of the previous week returned to me. My leaving do. The lovely food. My friends and the lovely presents. I let out a silent scream. I struggled to find the words as the realisation hit me: 'Oh my goodness, I'm now unemployed!'

I had given myself a couple of weeks to rest and recharge my batteries, before I began looking for work again, as I needed the break and time to reflect, before jumping into another role. I also knew I needed to have a regular income since my redundancy package would not last forever. Later that day I went out and explored the various recruitment agencies as I never had the need of one before; especially, since, from the age of sixteen, I had never been out of work. With that plan, I knew what I was looking for in my next job or employer and was not about to rush into anything.

I found two agencies based in the City near Liverpool Street Station and they were very keen to have me on their books. Their offices were near each other, so I saw them both on the same day. It was really funny, whenever you registered with an agency, the first thing they asked was if you were registered with anyone else. I said no to both because I wanted to see how they would serve me. I completed an online application and an automated test of my Microsoft knowledge and skills which would help match me with a potential employer. To ensure I capitalised on any opportunity, I spread my reach by registering with as many agencies as I could across London.

At one agency, based in East London, I came face-to-face with an older woman in a boutique consultancy. She was the owner, receptionist and secretary - a true one-woman band. I had made an appointment and, was invited to attend the registration. When I informed her, I had registered with her over the phone and gave her my name, the look on her face was not dissimilar to the one the co-author had when we met. She went through the registration process, asking me questions about my experience, the jobs I had undertaken and what I was looking for in my next role. My computer skills were then tested on a stand-alone desktop. She asked how many words per minute I could type but since I had not typed for a while, I said I was rusty but could do around fifty/fifty-five wpm. She then placed a sheet of paper on the desk for me to type. I looked at the neatly typed paragraphs and smiled, this was the kind of typing I liked, lengthy passages where I could just let my fingers glide over the keyboard. And with a few minutes left, I completed the test. She was surprised, since I had finished before the timer alarmed. She studied the paper and after a while asked if I knew how well I had done. I said I had not. She went on to say that my typing speed was recorded at eighty-six wpm. I was surprised as she was shocked, she clearly had not expected me to hit that type of speed and, to be honest, neither had I. Needless-to-say, I got a two-week placement in a recruitment agency near Liverpool Street Station and was grateful for that experience. The two agencies I had registered with gave me part-time placements in both Lehman Brothers and Deutsche Bank - the same banks I had applied to previously when I had first started looking for other banking jobs. It worked out in such a way, that the agencies scheduled my assignments so that when I finished at Lehman Brothers on a Friday, I would start at Deutsche Bank, the following Monday.

The Favoured Few

I enjoyed working in both banks, and it was while I was finishing up on an assignment at Lehman Brothers, when I received a phone call asking me to make my way to see the HR Director. I was nervous, wondering why I was being summoned. I had previously met the HR Director twice, and that was over a two-day period, whilst I was covering for her Executive Assistant, who had been off sick.

The HR Director introduced herself and said, "I've called you up here because I understand that you're a qualified trainer and have been working within training and development for some time." She went on to say, "Alison is about to go on maternity leave for four months and I wondered whether you were interested in covering her role while she was away."

I was surprised, I never expected to be in a training environment so soon outside of where I had previously worked, and as a qualified trainer too! I took the offer and it was a great opportunity and experience for me as I relished every day of that four-month maternity cover. It was my first 'real' training role and everything I had learned, was immediately put to good use - I needed to hit the ground running to prepare for an upcoming a large training event.

Once, while working with the Capital Markets trading team as a temporary staff member, I was encouraged to look through and apply for permanent or ongoing roles within the department. I expressed my interest to Lorraine who headed up the temporary staff applications. I was warned by other staff members, that Lorraine had her favourites, knowing this information, I applied anyway but it took a while before I heard anything.

One day, Lorraine happened to be on our trading floor and was walking towards me. I was about to say something when she walked straight pass me, without any acknowledgment. I thought it rude, but gave her the benefit of the doubt, waiting until she returned where I could ask about my application. As she was going by, I called out to her. She stopped, turned facing me with an exasperated look and said, "Yes Jacqui?" Before I could say anything further, she turned and walked away, saying over her shoulder, "I'm really busy, I can't talk now." I was flabbergasted, especially as everyone throughout the office had heard. To add insult to injury, she walked to the other side of the office and proceeded to stand and talk to one of the executive assistants there. I was livid and maybe it showed a little as I felt many eyes on me as if waiting to see a 'mad Black woman'. You know the one to which I refer? The Black woman who got aggressive when she did not like what anyone said to her or who intimidated those who crossed her. Well, as far as I was concerned that was not me because she doesn't exist!

A secretary who sat next to me, asked if I was okay. I said I was fine and continued typing an agenda. It was to be posted outside the meeting room where Lorraine so happened to be chatting. I printed the sheet and walked to the panel by the meeting room door. As I did so, Lorraine looked up and when she saw it was me, turned away, continuing to talk. As I placed the new agenda in the placeholder, she walked over and proceeded to try and apologise to me. I was not having any of it. Staring at her, speaking in a very low tone I said, "How dare you speak to me in that manner, it was totally unwarranted."

She tried to speak but I interrupted, "I'm totally disgusted at your behaviour. Please forget about even having a conversation with me, I'm no longer interested in the role."

I returned to my desk without saying anything, to anyone. It felt good, I was in control and was not angry. I had not given them that privilege. Lorraine, on the other hand, seemed traumatised at what had just happened since she stood by the meeting room long after I had left. When she finally moved, her body language looked like she was defeated. Her shoulders seemed to have slumped.

As it was my last week, I had no other assignments with Lehman Brothers, instead, another assignment came up with Deutsche Bank. I was really pleased because the incident with Lorraine had left me unsettled and I needed to leave that environment. I had not noticed it, but I heard the rumours of how Lorraine treated temporary staff, so confirming it was an attitude and behaviour she already had. Anyway, a few months later I bumped into one of the secretaries who had sat next to me at Lehman Brothers, she said that after my incident with Lorraine, all those who had seen and heard that day, complained to senior management about her behaviour. It transpired other people had been treated the same way I was. Fortunately, she was later made redundant. I would like to think that it was because of the incident between us that resulted in her going and I was sure if she had continued, the agencies would have probably heard and stopped sending temps there anyway.

I never worked at Lehman Brothers again but I was grateful for the experience, and continued working at Deutsche Bank for a few more months. By now, I had been temping for two years and felt ready for a permanent role. I was eventually offered a role in an electronic brokering business near Tower Bridge. It was my first role as a global learning and performance trainer, and I was very excited.

Apart from the incident with Lorraine, I had some pretty good experiences and was grateful for those opportunities. I did however learn not to take things at face value, as well as being mindful of how others saw me. The incident with Lorraine, taught me a valuable lesson in keeping my temper in check because, at the end of the day, we were like actors on a stage where the audience was always watching. Even though I faced these challenges throughout the duration of my assignments, I always ensured that I did my best in whatever role I was assigned, and the positive and supportive feedback the agencies always confirmed this. I had always aimed to be my true self and by using my emotional intelligence in everything I said and did helped me to step back and reflect on the situations that arose. Having this discerning spirit was essential as I progressed in my career.

Chapter 9 - After the Feast Came the Famine

*"Life has many ways of testing a person's will,
either having nothing happen at all or by
having everything happen all at once."*
~ Paulo Coelho ~

As I made my way to my new office, I was getting good at travelling but hated whenever the underground had its problems. Travelling to work on my first day I was early and as I sat on the overhead train I thought about my career and the places I had worked to date. I was pleased. My résumé was looking quite prestigious and where I was now heading was a far cry to where I had worked before. It was a subsidiary with links to electronic brokering, news and financial data reporting. The parent company was in the United States with offices in France and Switzerland. I felt I could grow in this the new role.

When I arrived, a young lady met me and said I would enjoy working in the company since it was fun there. I was introduced to the HR manager and the trainer I would be co-delivering with. They welcomed me to the team and I explained what kind of training I had done before. I was shown along a wide corridor where I would be working. It was strange to be situated in such a place but as I settled in, I accepted it, thinking it was just a temporary placement. I was shown around the building by the trainer and introduced to everyone else in the company. This was so different from where I previously worked since it would only be the immediate team I met on the first day; everyone else would be known to me over the coming weeks and months.

The very first person I was introduced to was the Managing Director's executive assistant, who then, introduced me to the MD himself. He was lovely, almost grandfatherly and so down to earth. We shook hands and, before I left his office, he said, "If you need to talk about anything, my door's always open."

That was a very nice for a boss of any organisation to say to a staff member on their first day and, I took up that offer with him later on down the road. As this was a small business and the building not too big, we met everyone quite quickly, and while walking with the trainer, I noted that there was only one other Black person throughout the entire company - myself and the HR officer. Two Black women in a workforce of two hundred and sixty people.

As a new employee, I needed to attend the inductions and when I arrived, I met both the HR manager and trainer. I thought it was unusual for a HR manager to be involved but noted the practice. As soon as the induction was over, the office became busy in preparation for the next batch of new employees (induction was held every two weeks) and a lot of work needed to be done. The weeks flew and though I was keen to start training, for some reason I was never given the opportunity. Soon, the next induction loomed, and I was hoping that at least I would be given the chance to co-deliver this time, so I asked the trainer. She looked uncomfortable. She said it was down to the HR manager as to when she felt I was ready. This annoyed me as I felt I was just seen and treated as a junior trainer with little or no experience. I made a mental note to see the HR manager to find out for myself. Fortune favoured me as a few days later she accidently deleted an entire document from her laptop. She panicked, not knowing what to do as I happened to walk into the office and found both the Black female HR officer and trainer peering over her shoulder. I asked if I could help. The HR manager seemed irritated and snapped, "Only if you've got a background in IT."

I answered yes and that I had gained a teacher's diploma in information technology while temping. I said I was also trained as a systems administrator then a brief stint as an IT trainer. All three ladies stared at me in disbelief, as if they could not believe a word I had just said yet I had long become used to this whenever I mentioned anything about my skills and qualifications.

"Would you like me to look at it for you?" I kindly asked.

The HR manager said, "Okay, but I've called IT so you may as well wait until one of them gets here to have a look at it."

When I looked at the laptop I realised what she had inadvertently done and retrieved the document in its entirety. By the time the IT guy arrived the problem was resolved and she was back working. She apologised to the technician for not ringing to cancel and in so doing, omitted to give me the credit for sorting the problem. It bothered me a little, but I was just glad to be of service. It also gave me an early warning signal that the HR manager would bypass me when necessary, especially with things I was more than capable of doing. I guess I may have been seen as a threat, especially with my IT knowledge and systems background.

The next induction day was very close and I ensured I knew the training material. The day arrived and I was ready, packaging the material for the taxi when it arrived. I dropped them into the cab and as I did, the trainer and HR manager climbed in. As I was about to do the same the HR manager said, "Jacqui, I think you should stay in the office and take calls from any of the late or lost new employees, redirecting them, if they should turn up here."

I could not speak. There had been no indication that I was not attending or not co-facilitating this induction and I stood rooted to the spot, watching as they drove away. It was obvious that the HR manager did not want anything to change. In fact, she wanted to deliver training at every opportunity she could. For me, I was employed to train but was relegated to undertake administrative work, fetching and carrying papers. It confirmed to me that mentioning my qualifications and knowledge had indeed made her feel insecure. After the incident where I managed to retrieve her deleted document, she ensured that any further IT problems in the office, she was either informed first or it was reported and logged directly with the IT Department. I only found this out when I bumped into the IT guy, one day. I asked, more problems? He responded yes - this is the third time this week! Personally, I thought it was a waste of time because I knew he was being called in for the most trivial of problems that could easily have been resolved without his intervention.

When I reached home, I thought about something Lola told me once. She said that in every job I had there would always be that one person who would have a problem with me. I asked why she said that since I was not a bad person. She had said it was not because I was horrible or anything like that, it was because my many skills threatened others. At the time I felt her statement was unfair and that she was being judgmental but eventually, I came to realise that what she had told me was true and it would only get worse. I was dejected, thinking maybe I had made a big mistake in joining this organisation, even though I liked working there and the people were nice enough. I wanted to be a trainer and did not want to leave but how was I going to accomplish that, especially with the way things were going with the HR manager.

Something needed to give that much I knew, and the very next day, I made my way to the HR office to see what further work was available. As I entered, the HR manager said good morning as if nothing had happened the day before. The trainer also said good morning but looked unhappy. In fact, she looked embarrassed, failing to make eye contact. I said nothing and asked if anything needed my attention. I knew it made no difference if I said anything about being left out and the HR manager proceeded to thank me for sending the misplaced new joiners. I also knew that if I had said something, it would have been deemed as sour grapes.

This "proving" my worth and competence as a trainer to the HR manager went on for a while and I felt I would never get a chance to do what I was hired to do but I was about to get my lucky break.

A series of corporate meetings with the managing director and other directors had been organised and the HR manager needed to attend all of them. The dates for these corporate meetings coincided with the induction dates, making her unavailable to do any further training. I was then told that I would be co-delivering. I was elated, I finally had my chance to do the job I was employed to do. The HR manager finally stepped back and the trainer, and I took over.

Everything worked well for a year, then a new HR director was recruited and he became the line manager to the HR manager. As soon as he joined, things began to change. An organisational restructure took place, reducing its size and for me, my role increased, and I was delivering the corporate inductions, conducting training sessions and working with other trainers in other parts of the global organisation. Soon, though, the HR manager decided she wanted to move on. This was not a problem at all, it was what happened after she left. The HR director decided to bring in his own people which included a trainer and, I felt apprehensive. It felt like I was in a B-movie, with me as the only black person in a group of people, walking around a creepy building and who most definitely was going to be the first one obliterated!

I began doing certain duties which was not on my job description. On one occasion, the HR director said he felt I was not qualified enough to do my job and went on to say that his previous staff were more suitably competent to undertake this role. I was stunned and needed no bigger indicator that he did not want me doing any form of training, and before long, I found myself relegated to doing just inductions. Yet, undeterred, I found other avenues in other departments where my skills were gratefully utilised. One of which was the Compliance Department. I was so grateful to Geoff, the director, and Pip, the compliance administrator, who allowed me to support them. This was a great distraction and confidence booster for me.

Knowing I could be potentially replaced added more pressure on me so, I decided to have a conversation with the managing director. In the meeting, I explained how I felt. Although he was empathetic, there was nothing he could really do to change my situation because of the wider changes happening throughout the organisation. It seemed, unbeknown to me, there was a lot more was going on. Even so, he moved me from the corridor and into an office with a new line manager. This meant I was still doing the inductions but, I was also being used for other training as well as liaising with the training teams across the entire organisation. It also meant that I got the chance to travel to the Paris office! Everything seemed to be on an even keel but unbeknownst to any of us in the office or even the department, darker forces outside of anyone's control, were to have an impact on everything. Not only within my organisation and all global financial institutions, but throughout the entire world.

I was on annual leave, visiting my family, and happened to be in my brother's photographic shop and studio, in his downstairs office. My brother had some new software he needed installing, and a few administrative tasks. I was down there for the best part of the day with no mobile phone signal and was not expecting any calls. On leaving my family to make my way home, I was in my car, just checking my phone to see if I had any missed calls. Pip, had rang several times, leaving frantic messages. Now I had the chance, I called her straight-away. She answered and what she said next shocked and scared me to my core. While I was in my brother's office, the World Trade Centre's Twin Towers had been hit by two airplanes. As she described the event she asked if I was near a TV, I said no but was making my way home. September 11th, 2001 or 9/11, would be remembered for so many reasons. The atrocity affected every single person and business, ours being no exception. Everything, it seemed, had been shut down overnight. The financial world's nervous system was alarmed and in order to preserve its vital functions, finances were syphoned from non-essential areas such as training, resulting in redundancies.

I was made redundant for a second time and as I was the last person recruited, I was the first to go. I suppose the HR director finally got his wish of getting rid of me. But, all forms of recruitment were immediately suspended, so he was unable to bring in any of his people either. In fact, the opposite began to happen as companies across the Square Mile began to downsize.

Later on, I sat with my line manager in a meeting and we talked about my redundancy options. He proposed that I should undertake further study, even though the qualifications I had gained so far had served me well, I now needed to get a degree, especially if I wanted to further my career. I was made redundant and left the organisation after two years and as part of my package, they paid for the first year of a two-year degree. So once again, I was unemployed. I also bought myself a leaving gift to celebrate, symbolising my time there. After my first redundancy I had purchased a beautiful mahogany writing desk with green leather and gold inlaid top and two matching leather chairs; one which swiveled. It cost a pretty penny but was so worth it. I wanted to reward myself for a great job I knew I had done.

The global situation was now frightening and very uncertain and because of this people were scared to fly anywhere. I took advantage of this by booking a flight for my daughter and I to go to Jamaica and spend some time with my mother. It was not until I arrived in Jamaica and began to unwind and relax, did I realise I had been working for a long time, without having a proper holiday. The odd day off here or there was not the same as taking a proper break. The first couple of days in Jamaica I woke up, looking catatonic. I was so tired and not with it, that even my mother took one look at me and said, "Go and lie down and rest." It took me three whole days before I could really feel or be myself again.

An Oasis in the Desert

Now that I was unemployed again, I needed to find another job pretty quickly, as yet again, my redundancy payout was not going to last. So, I signed with an agency knowing I would find a temporary, permanent or administrative job but would be happy as long as I was successful in securing something. 9/11 had made jobs scarce and even the temping ones were few and far between, even training roles were harder to come by. Nobody was hiring, so I applied for secretarial work and even that proved to be a problem. At home, my bills were mounting, some were almost astronomical. Every day, I would call the agency to find out if any roles were available but, the answer would always be the same - no suitable jobs were being offered.

A few months in I immersed myself into my studies, my redundancy money keeping us afloat. It was after six months' that things started getting tighter and I limited the use of the internet (a dial-up rather than today's broadband). And every day when I spoke with the recruitment consultant the answer was always the same: *"I'm sorry there're no suitable roles available for you."* Soon, I became really desperate. It felt like I was in the desert, dry and barren, with no sign of an oasis for miles. I felt despondent and in despair, the thought of another bill falling on my doormat making me even more apprehensive.

I thought about the agency, and the fact that even though I had built a relationship with the consultant, she never once called me to let me know they were still looking on my behalf or if there was anything on their books for me. There was just silence and the more I thought about it, the more resentful I became. I began to feel that the roles they had were not for the likes of me. I came to this conclusion because people were being hired, temporary roles being filled and even a couple of my work colleagues who were made redundant, managed to secure temp roles.

One morning I was sitting at my laptop, in my pyjamas, typing my next assignment. The great thing about my university lecturers was that they knew about my dilemma and, were very empathetic towards me. I was grateful for their patience as I was uncertain if I could have endured additional pressure. I called my recruitment consultant and asked if anything had come in. She answered, yet again, "I'm sorry Jacqui, there's nothing that's suitable." I snapped and said, "I've been calling you for months and each time we've spoken it's been the same response. If I'm wasting my time calling you, please do let me know and I won't call again."

She started reassuring me that this was not the case, and that there were just no suitable jobs around that matched my skills. I was uninterested in what she had to say but thanked her anyway. I was really annoyed, *if they had no roles coming in, how were they staying afloat as a business?* I assumed that a chosen few were being given these roles, an assumption yes, I know, but I was right! I could see jobs being advertised on the internet and in job sections of the various free London newspapers that this agency had been advertising in, but I was not offered any of them. I was resentful that the agency I cared to sign with had not valued me or my skills enough to find a placement for me.

The next day just after completing my assignment my phone rang, it was the consultant. I would like to think that our previous day's conversation had pricked her conscience and forced her to actively look for a suitable role for me and, having found one, decided to call with some good news. It was. She had secured a one-day assignment with one of the big four financial institutions. She even asked if I wanted it. I said, "One day was better than no days." She asked how soon I could get there. I replied I could be there by noon. She said she would let them know I was on my way. I was overjoyed. I had finally secured a temp job. I was back working even if it was for just one day. There was a clash with my university assignment so, I rang my tutor and told her what had happened, and I was permitted to drop the completed assignment the following day.

I was so excited when I arrived for the work, anyone would have thought it strange for a temp to be so keen and cheerful, even asking for more tasks to do It was an oasis, not a mirage but the real thing and, I was taking a long drink from the cool water in the shade of its palm trees. *A bit over the top, but I had been unemployed for nine months so just roll with me with these analogies.* By the end of the day the manager asked if I could return the next day; then at the end of that following day, I was asked if I could return on the next day. I was relishing being asked to return each time. But about an hour before leaving for home I was approached by the manager and told that, unfortunately, they could not keep me on as the lady whose role I had been covering was returning after the weekend.

The manager asked me, "Did you enjoy your time here?"

"Yes, and I also like the organisations culture too."

"Would you work here again?"

I said, "I would."

"Well, I hope you get something soon. Thank you for your hard work while with us," she said.

I was just pleased to have done a good job and having the one-day stretch into three. As I left, my phone rang. It was the agency who had placed me and this time it was the manager and not the consultant. He congratulated me on a job well done and informed me that I had been given an ongoing contract with that same organisation. I was so excited that felt as if I was floating on my way to Waterloo Station. I had finally made it out of the desert.

Nothing had prepared me for my time in the wilderness and it had been a dark and dismal time, but I knew I would carry on regardless, not just for myself but for my family. I now had a young daughter who depended on me and her father and it was my responsibility and duty of care to keep her secure. I determined to succeed and needed to be resilient and patient while waiting for the opportunity that would lead me to another adventure.

Chapter 10 - Playing with the Big Boys

*"So many of our dreams at first seem
impossible, then they seem improbable,
and then, when we summon the will, they
soon come back inevitable."*
~ Christopher Reeve ~

It took me only three days to show the manager my skills were what they needed in the company. Ironic. After all the time I had been religiously phoning the consultant and being told there was nothing for me, I got her to see things from my perspective, prompting her to get me an assignment the very next day. So, here I was, starting an ongoing assignment with the same organisation I had been placed at for only one day! I half expected the consultant to call and congratulate me or something since we had built a nine-month relationship but to be honest, I was not that bothered as I was far too happy about starting a new adventure

I was placed in Banking & Capital Markets as their secretarial support to a senior manager and two junior accountants. One day, the senior manager or Regional Knowledge Leader and I were having a discussion, talking about the work she needed me to do. I informed her of my training background and on hearing this, she offered me a fulltime role as a Knowledge Officer, the paperwork being completed before the day's close of business.

The Knowledge Platform

I was no longer a temp, but a new employee and I still could not believe I had been at home, in front of my computer, in my pyjamas, feeling forlorn at the prospect of having to scrape through more days, weeks and months without a job. I was thankful and offered up prayers of gratitude to the Almighty for taking me through my trials and tribulations. Now in work, this was to be another new experience for me and once I became familiar with the different systems, I could deliver workshops and conduct inductions.

All was going well, when I learnt of the merging with the Knowledge Management Services team. It was to be headed up by someone else and, initially, I felt aggrieved since my boss was the one who had offered me the role. I later found out that my boss and the management were unable to get on, so she chose to move on, and it was not long before there were rumours about redundancies. This made it a hat-trick of redundancies for me and I prepared as best as I could. Soon the confirmation came and we were called into a meeting but pre-empting it, I had packed my belongings just to be ready to leave. But, I was to learn that the changes were about departments' merging their knowledge and skills into one and not about redundancies. I was not exactly relieved since I envisaged treating myself to another leaving gift from Selfridges! Yet, it was not long before I was on the move again and this time, I hoped it would be for the last time as I was beginning to feel like a nomad.

The day I joined this new team, I knew it was not going to be easy working there, because of the conversation with my New Zealander line manager; she knew all about me and what I was doing with my studies. This unsettled me. At one stage, I thought she was asking far too many personal questions, but I answered them not wanting to appear rude. By now, I had completed my post graduate Diploma in Human Resource Strategies and decided to continue studying for a Master of Arts degree. She knew this too and said, "I heard you've just completed your post graduate studies, congratulations."

"Thank you," I answered.

She then asked, "Are you going to do your master's degree?"

I said, "Yes, I'm planning to."

She said, "I've a diploma in adult education."

I found it strange of her to volunteer information and for some reason, it felt like she was gathering intel on me. I knew then that my fate was sealed. It was not just about her questions. It was the motive behind the questioning; which became a lot clearer soon enough.

I was quite ambitious along my career journey and, had built good relationships with the partners in the industry groups since my role was two-fold. I was a knowledge officer, so building relationships was important as well as being an internal consultant ensuring all the staff and new joiners were adequately trained and competent on the organisation's knowledge platform and systems. As an employee, bonuses were dependent upon good appraisal scores and I had received some glowing references. So, when the time came for submission, I completed the appraisal form, putting the feedback I had received plus my own comments and self-assessment as to what grade I felt I had achieved. I submitted this for my line manager and the senior manager's comments before having it signed off with HR. I knew I had worked extremely hard to achieve the good feedback and was expecting a wonderful reward.

At the appraisal meeting with my line manager, I was not prepared for the comments and the overall score she and the senior manager gave me. In my own assessment I felt I had reached a Level 5 which meant a good bonus but, what they wrote overshadowed the glowing feedback I had received. They both gave me a two which meant I was not eligible for a bonus and would need further development. I was flabbergasted and queried their marks. Her response was non-committal. I said I felt their scoring did not reflect the feedback I had been given and it was unfair that they were ignored. I was upset and disgusted that these two women were using the appraisal system to keep me in my role without any hope of getting a bonus or even progressing. I tried reasoning with my line manager. but she just said that they had made their decision and it was final. She then invited me to sign the form. I refused. I was angry. She said that it would not matter what I thought or the fact that I had not signed the form, it was still going to be a Level 2 and that was that.

As I left the room, I felt nauseous and dizzy and by the time I returned to my desk, my head was pounding. The senior manager who was at her desk, did not even look up at me. I needed air and just wanted to leave the building. In the office, it felt as if I was choking, the air suddenly feeling contaminated. In the sunshine I deeply inhaled the fresh air as I walked along the bridge on the River Thames. I walked past City Hall, turning back at London Bridge and towards the office. For the entire time, I wondered why I was being treated this way. A direct guillotine drop, chop and the clean lopping of my head. I needed to go home and not think about the whole thing and just tried my best to relax. On my return to the office, I picked up my belongings and left without saying a word to anyone. As soon as I reached home, I called my friend. She was a Knowledge Manager in one of the industry groups. We spoke about my appraisal and the score they wanted to give me, despite the positive feedback. As we talked, I cried until I was spent. She listened, then advised me to get a good nights' sleep and in the morning have one more conversation with my line manager and if she was still adamant, and would not budge on the scoring; then I should go to HR. The very next morning I woke early. I was still upset but with my friend's advice ringing in my ears, I knew I needed to stay calm when having a discussion with my line manager. As soon as I arrived at work I asked if we could discuss my appraisal scores. In the meeting room, the first thing she said was, "I'm not changing the mark we gave you, if that's what you wanted to discuss."

I said, "Yes, that's exactly what I wanted to discuss as I would like to know how you came by that score, seeing as all the feedback I received was glowing and should've given me a four or five mark. I can't understand why the two of you gave me that score which meant I won't receive a bonus."

She stared at me for a while before saying, "Because we felt you still had developmental needs."

I responded, "In what areas do I need this development?"

She could not answer and I added "I'm not going to sign the form and I'll be taking it to HR."

She heatedly answered, "You do that!"

I left and went straight to HR. There I spoke with an officer, asking if they could identify where my developmental needs were. The officer said she would need to speak to both my senior and line manager because she was unable to comment. It took another day before I found out the result of the conversations between my manager, senior manager and HR. Eventually, I was called into the HR office and told by the officer that my line manager and senior manager would not give me a four or a five scoring but compromised to give me a three. I was enraged and said that everything was a complete farce. The HRO looked really embarrassed since she knew that it was all wrong but could not go against management. It was made it quite clear to me that if I did not take the scoring, I would receive nothing at all. So, I accepted the three score, receiving a paltry 1% pay increase which would have probably paid for my weekly shopping without any change. As I write this, I clearly see the systematic and deliberate practice in widening the ethnicity pay gap, which was wrong on so many levels.

I felt betrayed and deflated but I was not going to let these two women treat me like I was rubbish. A little while later, I heard that the same HR officer went on long-term sick leave, due to the stress she had been under within the workplace. This was wrong from every angle, but it was very much 'do as you're told or you're out of a job' scenario, I think.

While this entire debacle was taking place I was studying for my master's degree and my situation affected my focus. It really impacted me whilst I was typing up my dissertation. The negative experiences staying with me as I mulled over and tried to make sense of everything; from the probing questions, to the fraudulent appraisal and my line manager having the nerve to ask if I was still studying for my master's degree. I felt like I had been sucker-punched; with her deliberate tactics that showed she was doing her best to hamper my career and university progress. To be honest, her oppressing me in this manner was the first time I came up close-and-personal with professional jealousy. I knew I was more qualified than her and by the looks of it, more experienced. By denying me my true score, it was the only way they could keep me back and so far, it had worked.

After that day, I said very little to either manager, unless it was work related and about supporting staff or junior accountants. A few months later I received a phone call from my friend - the Knowledge Manager - she wanted to meet up and needed to speak with me away from the office. I thought that was strange but agreed, nonetheless. We met in a nearby coffee shop and, she basically confirmed what I had always suspected, that my career was being deliberately blocked and that the two managers I worked with were totally out of order, using their positions to hold me back. She said she was leaving the organisation for another big job and, although her boss was sorry to see her go, he had asked her who she felt would be a good replacement. She had given my name and said that I was more than competent to take over her role. Though I was happy for her, I was flattered she had recommended me. She said that my boss – the senior manager - was approached by her boss, who was a partner in the firm, he asked her if I could be released to undertake the role. The senior manager told him no, asking him to choose someone else from the knowledge management team. The partner was so shocked and outraged that he told my friend. I felt sick as she told me. I was hurt that these two women were abusing their powers to stop me from progressing. What was even worse, I knew I had done nothing to warrant this type of treatment. First it had been my appraisal and now a new job opportunity. I felt like I had been given a life sentence without parole and as long as I stayed in the organisation, I would be locked in with no prospect of release.

I decided to confront the senior manager because I was not going to waste my time speaking to my line manager and as soon as I returned to the office., I calmly asked if I could have a word. She smiled and said yes of course. The thing which I could not get over was that the pair of them had this type of synchronicity between them as if they were twins but then, they were both similar- they both had long blond hair and blue eyes. The only difference being - one was an American and the other - a New Zealander.

We went into a meeting room and I gave her both barrels. "Why did you block my opportunity to move into a knowledge manager role?"

She was astonished at my approach and angrily answered, "I didn't."

I said, "Yes you did, the partner was appalled at what you'd said, that he told the knowledge manager who then told me. Why would you do that?"

She replied, "Everyone likes you in the role you're doing. You're doing it so well."

I retorted, "I'm doing it well? My appraisal didn't reflect that. I don't think you believe that I've got goals and aspirations of my own?"

She just glared and said she felt that I was not ready for a managerial role and needed more experience. This comment ended our discussion. I had gotten her riled, a bit like a "rabbit in the headlights" scenario, because she had not expected me to confront her. She was really mad, and I could tell she would somehow make me pay. For me, whatever she did would ultimately determine whether I stayed or left the organisation. I knew she had friends in HR who she could influence or block any job applications I made, and this was exactly what she did! She manipulated the situation to the point where the role the partner wanted me for, was downgraded. So even if I had gotten it, there would have been no promotion or salary increase. This was overt and not covert bullying since they were doing this with the knowledge that there was not a thing, I could possibly do about it. Eventually, but not before I received the invitation to attend an interview, my line manager decided to have a pep talk with me.

She said, "Don't feel you've to leave if you don't get offered the job Jacqui?"

I calmly responded, "Oh no, I won't be leaving at all; there's a big difference between applying for a job and someone asking for you personally to join their team. I won't be going anywhere." Even though I was relaxed, I was very angry but did not make it show.

I smiled. Although it was a farcical situation, I felt victorious knowing I was wanted and, even though I did not end up getting the job, I knew I had been the first choice for the partner. By now, everyone in the office knew what had happened with me and my managers blocking me and because of that fiasco, the senior manager was moved to another part of the organisation. It was not a demotion; it was more like being banished from the kingdom. As for my line manager, as soon as things started to look bad, she quickly jumped ship to work in another department. Shortly after, I moved too and by then I had gained my master's degree. It was a bittersweet feeling because I knew my career had been stunted.

I half-heartedly applied for another role - a Global Knowledge Manager – but was still smarting from my previous experience. It was offered to me, but my heart was not in it and I was not as enthusiastic as I should or could have been. In fact, I did not want the job. What I needed was a fresh challenge, so I began looking for external jobs. I was no longer happy in my role of a knowledge officer, even though I had really enjoyed the work, especially the interaction and development of staff; I had been treated unfairly and I could not stay to be further demotivated.

Eventually, I saw an online job advertisement, so I applied. I was invited to attend an assessment centre, so I took a day off and went along to a hospital in West London. I had no idea that when I had applied that the role was working in the National Health Service (NHS) because the job advertisement did not actually specify who the recruiting organisation was. I knew nothing about the NHS, but I prepared as best as I could.

The first part of my interview was feedback from an online assessment I had completed prior. It came from a senior manager of the department where I would be working; if successful. The next stage was to give a presentation on performance management using their appraisal system, which I knew nothing about. Thankfully I was able to tap into my sister's knowledge who by then, had worked for many years within the healthcare industry. I had my presentation in front of a panel of four interviewers it was also going to be filmed - so no pressure really. Anyway, I asked the panel to be gentle with me since I was unfamiliar with the NHS. Unfortunately, there were technological challenges as the laptop I was to use, failed to function. One of the panel members who would be a part of the team I was being interviewed for, struggled to get it ready for me; he was so apologetic. While I wondered whether this was part of the interview process, a test to see how I coped under stress or issues that arose. But I was well prepared and used copies of my presentation as handouts. It was an interesting day and as I returned home, I hoped I was successful. I had even forgot about been filmed.

Back in my old job, I think management knew it was only a matter of time before I actually left. They were not wrong because exactly one week after the interview and assessment process, I was offered the job. I was overjoyed. I was venturing into unchartered territory. A move into the healthcare industry after spending twenty-three years in the corporate world and I was so looking forward to it.

Looking back, whilst employed, I realised that in all of the organisations, there was this endemic misuse of power and unprofessional behaviour that was the norm. There were many hard knocks and setbacks along the way, but I never allowed it to stop me from achieving my goals or gaining my degrees. I truly believe that without my firm foundation in faith, a loving family and supportive network of friends, I could not have overcome the trials and tribulations I had faced. There was a boldness within me I never envisaged I could have attained, enabling me to look past the malicious acts of individuals and gain a leverage that helped me to progress towards my goals. All I could do was be the best I could be in all that I did. Another thing that helped me tremendously was being able to forgive those who had treated me unfairly and unjustly, as this was the only way I could have moved forward, otherwise I would have been letting all the issues and gripes live rent-free in my head and heart. This would have done me no good whatsoever, so it was best to forgive and move on. It certainly worked for me!

Chapter 11 - The Imperial Way

*"Nothing happens until the pain of remaining
the same outweighs the pain of Change."*

~ Arthur Burt ~

So here I was in a new role, new organisation and new adventure. I had never worked in the healthcare industry before, so this was a steep learning curve. At my interview I was told that within fourteen months the organisation was merging with two others, bringing the total workforce to around ten thousand staff. As soon as I arrived, my line manager wasted no time in introducing me to everyone and as part of my role, I was to line manage two white middle-aged men - Andrew and Simon. There were also two Black women who worked in the administrative office. They were both friendly and would share their knowledge on how things were done within the department. They would also ensure that the course materials and rooms were set up each day.

At the same time, another woman was also appointed, joining the team at the same level as me. I immediately recognised her as one of the participants at the assessment centre I had attended. I especially remembered her because she was a bit standoffish. I was getting into the flow of things as the organisation prepared for the merger and I was under no illusions about the major changes that were coming.

Deidre was unfriendly, even when I tried making light conversation, it was clear from her clipped responses that she was uninterested in any of my pleasantries. When we had applied for the job, neither one of us knew there were two vacancies that were advertised, one was permanent and the other, on contract. I got the permanent job. So, imagine when we were reintroduced to each other on her first day in the team; her energy was as false as her smile. I tried to ignore it, but I knew that something was going to happen between us. Call it an intuition if you would.

Our line manager felt that as a team we were skilled enough to have meetings without her being present and as soon as we did, Deidre started. At first, it was subtle comments but then she began to say unwarranted things like: *"You're not at one of the Big Four now Jacqueline,"* or, *"That may've worked in the City but we're not there now"*. But since there was a lot of work to do in preparation for the merger, we both behaved like professionals. I willingly shared my knowledge and experience but whatever I did, it seemed to annoy her, making our relationship even more strained. I did not have a clue as why and surmised it as good old professional jealousy. It never mattered how pleasant I was, she never engaged with me, only speaking to me if it had to do with work. A harmonious environment was a happy one, so, I had no illusion about us being pals, swapping recipes or even having lunch together but we needed to work together.

Andrew and Simon seemed to gravitate towards Deidre, conversing matters that we as a team should be discussing. For example, whenever I entered our office, they would be in deep conversation, switching as soon as I entered. If I caught a hint of what they were talking about and enquired, there would be a flimsy response, so I would accept it without further thought. I sensed they were talking about me and I was not being paranoid. Once, when Deidre approached me, querying something I had instructed Andrew and Simon to do, that was the red flag. I knew that they were going to her for support. If I asked them to do a task, they looked at me as if to say, *why don't you do it yourself.* This led me to believe that both of them resented being line managed by a Black woman. I would also say openly to them, in front of her, that they needed to come to me first, letting them know I was not going to put up with what they were doing. This seemed to be the case because in one way or the other, Deidre would challenge me on their behalf, but I would always let her know that what I asked for was required and would thank her for querying this on their behalf.

As the merger got closer, our programmes of work grew. Not only that, I was also getting closer to going on maternity leave since I was seven and half months pregnant and feeling tired a lot of the time. My second child was due a few months after the actual merger took place.

I was asked by my line manager to submit a proposal and conduct some workshops for the managers. On the day I handed in the proposal, Deidre, Andrew and Simon heard about it, and began asking questions as to why I was the one chosen to undertake this project, especially since I was about to go on maternity leave. This probing infuriated me. It seemed that Deidre was undermining me, especially because I was the only Black manager in the team. It also looked like it was okay for them to sit and discuss as well as question my decisions. It was obvious that they were annoyed or even angry that I had been chosen to undertake the project, but it required my background in web design as well as other skills. On that day, I told them it had already been accepted by management and without any further comment, walked out of the office, slamming the door behind me.

That was the first time I had actually encountered this type of hidden bullying, what I describe as a 'hive mode and mentality' in which they operated and approached as a unified body. Anyone reading this could argue that these individuals were only enquiring or were concerned because I was pregnant and it could have been too much for me but...no, I did not accept those arguments. From the day Deidre had arrived in the team, it was evident that she was collaborating with Andrew and Simon and they even went to her for line management support rather than come to me. If the roles were reversed and it had been three Black people asking those questions or even having their own meeting; they would have been hauled up in front of a senior manager with all sorts of accusations trumped up against them. This was not paranoia but facts and was still happening in all types of industries and organisations where Black people were employed in the UK.

Finally, I went on maternity leave handing over my incomplete projects to Deirdre. One of which, was the very same project I had been questioned about. On my return to work I was to do a presentation to the newly appointed managers in the newly merged organisation. This would take place twelve weeks after my son's birth and was doable since my mother was coming over from Jamaica to bond with and care for her tenth grandson. This gave me the opportunity to return to work as an external consultant.

Twelve weeks later I returned to work ready to deliver the programme. I had agreed a number of sessions and was looking forward to seeing my proposal come to fruition. Deidre was now acting manager as our line manager was on a sabbatical. When I arrived, I greeted everyone but noticed Deidre had not said anything and kept looking at me. I ignored her and asked no one in particular, what room I was conducting the training in. Andrew and Simon both responded saying they were unsure and that I should check with the admin staff. I thanked them. As I was walking towards the door. Deidre followed me, wishing to speak to me before I reached reception.

"Why are you here?" She asked, "You should be at home looking after your baby."

I stared at her, anger rising within me. I knew she disliked me and that she made no attempt to hide the fact, worse now that she was in charge. I calmly answered, "My son's fine, he's with his grandmother who flew over from the West Indies to spend time with her grandson. And, I'm here because my proposal was accepted by senior management."

I left her, heading towards the reception office. I was glad she had not followed me because I would have really struggled to keep my composure. In the reception office the ladies saw how incensed I was. They had witnessed Deidre and I in the foyer and I was sure the look on my face told them everything they needed to know but they greeted me warmly, asking about my son and how I was feeling. I relaxed and showed them photos of my son on my phone while enquiring about the room and Louanne - the junior of the two ladies - informed me that everything had been done and it was ready. Beatrice was the other office administrator.

Louanne and I had a great friendship, just like when I worked with Lola at the bank. This time, I was the senior manager and Louanne, a junior staff member. She told me everything that had happened since I had been on maternity leave. To be forewarned was to be forearmed, because all the things she said indicated that a lot was going on and it had started

immediately after our manager went on her sabbatical and I on maternity leave. It seemed that Deidre was on a power trip and that she was a tyrant who picked on Louanne and Beatrice for the most trivial of things. Louanne said she was fed up and wished she could leave but was unable to do because of her young daughter and the hours she worked suited her needs.

I conducted the training and found that the majority of the managers who were attending had no form of performance management training whatsoever. As a result of this, they failed to follow the policies and procedures, and were subsequently embroiled in all forms of bullying with harassment cases taken out against them. Out of the sixteen participants I trained that day, two-thirds were white managers and some of the stories they shared I could write a book.

After my run-in with Deidre, we never spoke to each other for the remainder of the training sessions I had booked. So, whenever I arrived, she was either in meetings or busy in her office with the door closed; that suited me fine. As for Andrew and Simon, I gave them a wide berth, after all they were "Team Deidre" and I was not going to challenge that setup. It was not an ideal situation, but I had gone past caring and was not going to fight them. So, I got on with my work and left the managing to Deidre especially since that was what she wanted. I later learned that Deidre had worked in the same company with Simon prior to joining the organisation.

My maternity leave was almost up, and I had secured a nursery place very close to where I took the underground, so it was easy to drop off and pick up my son. With this sorted I wondered how work would be when I returned and speaking with Louanne, I learnt that there always seemed to be some drama going on two or three times a week. Soon, though, I returned to work, doing what I had done before. I did not expect any major changes but was in for a shock. Andrew and Simon, my two direct reports, had metamorphosed from two white middle-aged men into two Black women! It was obvious. While I was away, Andrew, Simon and Deidre had built a case for her to be their line manager, instead of me. I did not know what was discussed to get this sanctioned by senior management, but they had. I did not challenge the setup or say anything to anyone on how I felt. Andrew and Simon were unhappy with having a Black female manager and they had consistently shown this. Was it an abuse of position, power and protocol? I would say it was but... it made no difference even if I had complained as the deed had already been done. There was another change in my work my project was not returned to me. In fact, my colleague was very insistent that he had worked hard on it and wanted the kudos. I did not fight that either. After all, I was the originator and had already trained staff and, in doing so fulfilled that dream.

Later on, there was more shocking news. My line manager was back from her sabbatical and was leaving the organisation. This came as no surprise since it had become untenable for her to stay. A lot of managers were vying for pole-position in the new organisational infrastructure, and she was not one of those managers who had been slotted into a new role. In fact, her role was the only one advertised externally whereas all the others had been guaranteed jobs.

It was sad to see her go, since she had been the first line manager who really took an interest in me and my development. A true people-person, who gave the support I needed to enhance my skills as well as recommending me to others, including senior management. Now, she was leaving. It was difficult losing such a significant person, since I had no other senior management support in my corner. It felt like I was now going to be fodder for the vicious wolves. Later, when we spoke, I deduced that it had not been her choice for her to go and I was apprehensive because I knew that there would be more challenges from Deidre. Yet, my line manager did one more glorious act for me before she left, by paying for my development and licensing on two programmes - The Springboard Women's Development and PRINCE2. She obviously knew I would not be given the chance to develop once she was gone and for that, I would always be grateful.

Under The Thumb

It did not take Deidre long to let me know who was in charge. You see, when someone disliked you for whatever reason and were in a position of power, they could use it to make the other persons' life a living hell. With Deidre, this was definitely the case; if I sighed too heavily, she would have had a problem with me. Yet, we worked as best as we could and as normal as possible. Eventually, a new member joined the team and Deidre felt that someone was needed to fill her vacant role especially since no suitable replacement had been found for the senior position she was deputising for. It was a smart move by her to appoint someone in her vacant position since this ensured that she stayed in her acting up position a little while longer.

Dave was the new member of staff who got on really well and integrated into the team quite seamlessly. One day, we were having a team meeting. Deidre was at a flipchart writing down all the contributions everyone offering up as ideas to take forward, all except mine. Whenever I offered an idea or solution, she failed to acknowledge me or write it on the flipchart. This happened three times and on the fourth time, Dave asked her to note it down. Reluctantly, she agreed, but I could tell she was annoyed. After the session we went to lunch and while there Dave started to ask me questions. It seemed her omission of my contributions had not gone unnoticed by him.

He asked, "I noticed there seems to be a problem between you and Deidre. What are you going to do about it?"

"I don't have a problem with her. Her problem is with me," I said. "I feel she doesn't like Black people and always picked faults in everything I did."

Well, who told me to say anything? He had been recruited by Deidre. They often lunched together, where I guess they discussed what happened in the office. Once, he had told her about something that Simon had done and she had been very swift in dealing with him. She acted like a school headteacher whenever she reprimanded anyone but with me, it was different and her bullying continued, becoming very petty. I so wanted to be out of that place.

One day I was at the photocopier and called the engineer because it was not working properly, but I had forgotten to put a note on it saying what I had done so. It was my work which had jammed it and Deidre came to me, accusing me of leaving it unworkable without calling out the engineer. She said how irresponsible I was since there were urgent documents she needed to print and send out. I explained the engineer had been called but she was not listening. She spoke over me but I just got on with my job, not listening in return. I apologised and told her I had mentioned it to everyone in the team that the engineer would be arriving soon. Unable to take it any further, she walked away. I knew she was angry and wanted to tear a couple more strips out of me but, instead, she walked away.

Things in the office got to the point where I was ready to quit and return to temping. I was being worn down by Deidre's incessant and unrelenting need to take her issues out on me at every given opportunity. There was no other recourse either because the Associate Director who was her line manager was the one who had appointed her. He also knew what was going on in the office since other members of the team had complained about Deidre, but nothing was done. At one stage I was so fed up, I applied and kept applying for any relevant job that was going, hoping to get lucky. Unfortunately, I did not receive one invitation for an interview. I felt broken, resigning myself to the fact that I was never going to leave and get away from this mistreatment.

One day, she seemed to be in a placid mood and happened to be in our eLearning room where I was speaking to a woman doing her training. The woman was saying her husband was a bit messy. I laughed and said that my husband disliked mess and was always tidying things away and, one day I had phoned him, asking where the stereo for the car was since he had tidied it away from where I would normally put it. We both laughed when I told her where I found it. As we were laughing, Deidre happened to be listening and said, "Not everyone has a perfect marriage like you Jacqueline!"

That took us by surprise. I had developed a knack of taking the sting out of her verbal attacks and merely said jovially that we did not have a perfect marriage and had our ups and downs like everyone else; the difference being in the making up. I then laughed and winked at her. She failed to find it funny, snorting as she left the room. The lady and I just stared at each other, raising our eyebrows. Another day, I was called into a one-to-one meeting with Deidre to go over project work. Everything seemed fine until she said, "You spoke to Dave and told him that I was a racist and a bully."

I was stunned. "I had done no such thing!"

Infuriated, she rose to her feet and repeated, "Yes you had, you told him I was a racist and a bully!"

"No, I hadn't said that to Dave. I'll tell you what, why don't we just ask him?"

I left her office, went to find Dave, returning to her office. I asked, "Dave, have I ever said to you that Deidre was a racist and a bully?"

Dave answered, "No."

"Okay, I'm going to ask you one more time. Dave at any time during the time you've worked here, have I ever said to you that Deidre was a racist and a bully?"

David answered again, "No, you never did."

I thanked him while looking at Deidre. "You were saying Deidre?"

She muttered under her breath but I caught what she had said; she said she thought Dave and her were friends. I terminated the meeting but pre-empted that Deidre would go to the Associate Director. I was certain she had fabricated the whole matter, to make it look like I was at fault. I tried calling the Associate Director but to no avail. I also felt that somehow Deidre had already given her side of the story and with the length of time it took for the AD to get back to me, confirmed it. After that episode, Dave started to get a taste of Deidre's wrath by being picked on for silly things. When he came to speak to me about it, all I could say was I was glad he could see what I had been going through.

When the AD finally spoke with me, she suggested it would be best if Deidre and I attended mediation and that she would organise it. In the mediation sessions it was like a military manoeuver. When the mediators asked what was happening between Deidre and I, and how we felt; Deidre said that as her line manager, she felt I had not given her the respect she felt she deserved. She said that whenever she came into the office in the mornings, she expected me to greet her with a smile! I kid you not. Control and command. The mediator explored a bit more, asking Deidre to give other examples of when she felt I was being insubordinate. The mediators said it was good manners to greet your boss with a smile in the mornings and saw nothing wrong with Deidre's request. I was appalled. It seemed that the mediation session was one-sided, as the mediator seemed to continually agree with Deidre's responses and requests. I could not understand why the mediator thought this was a reasonable request. Deidre also said I was unfriendly towards her and that I was not like that with other people in the office or external people who visited. I rolled my eyes in despair and said that I could not be friendly with someone who did not like me. She did not respond and that led me to think that she had some serious problems and it was not just about me. I had tried to be friendly with her, but it was not enough. At one point, I said I found her to be funny and asked if saying good morning and smiling, would make her happy. She said yes. Well, the mediator said, it was reasonable to try this new way of working for six weeks.

I was extremely unhappy. I was unsure for how long I could keep up the façade of being smiley just for Deidre, but I decided to play ball just the same. The difference, I was determined to get through the six weeks. We agreed we would both try and work together more harmoniously and with that an agreement was signed between us and the mediator. The session stipulated that we needed to be polite and courteous to each other...sorry scratch that, Deidre was the manager and therefore not at fault so, my interpretation of what had been said and agreed was only for her benefit. If I had not agreed, it would not have gone well and I would have looked like the aggressor. I was the one who was at fault or that was how they saw it. Anyway, we commenced the six-week trial and at first, I would spray on my smile each morning but by week three I genuinely beamed and would say good morning to Deidre. Why the sudden change? Well, I got to find out a bit more about her personal life.

On one rare occasion, when we actually talked civilly, discussing our families and children, she shared that there were two key fractured relationships in her life; both, beyond repair. Suddenly, I felt empathy. She had been married for a number of years and trapped in a relationship where she had no control, doing everything she was told to do. And the other was with her mother. It turned out that her mother was very critical of every decision she had ever made, whether it was for her career or otherwise. Suddenly, it appeared to me and I immediately understood why she was using her position to control others, including me. I realised it would take more than six weeks' mediation for us to come to grips with her own journey and how much it affected others.

By the time the six weeks were up, we were once again at the mediation office. The mediators asked Deidre how she felt the six weeks went and she responded that it was great, meaning I had done everything she wanted me to do without any cause for concern. She had no complaints because I was a 'model employee'. When the mediators asked me the same question, I said I had formulated things which I wanted to address before we finished and moved on, something which was not addressed at any time during the first mediation session. I said I felt the mediation service was being manipulated to suit Deidre's needs and that the real reasons why we ended up in mediation was because she had accused me of calling her a racist and bully and, in doing so, I still had a witness to prove this was a lie. So, it was in my best interest to actually address and vocalise, why for me the mediation process was a complete farce. I said Deidre had never actually apologised to me for falsely accusing me of calling her a racist and a bully and I was disappointed that the mediation service was being leveraged as a form of control. I think my words hit home, catching Deidre off-guard. She suddenly got defensive, saying she had not been in the role for long, to which I responded that eighteen months was long enough for any manager to fully understand their role, responsibilities and duty of care to the staff they managed.

She became agitated, her voice rising as she said, "As your line manager you need to do as I say." At this point the mediators jumped in and like me, probably thought she had lost control. They asked if I would accept an apology from Deidre and settle the dispute there and then. I said I would. Reluctantly, Deidre said she was sorry for accusing me but whether she meant it or not, I did not know. I accepted her apology and the mediation concluded. I accepted it because I had already forgiven her, not because she deserved it but because I needed peace of mind and more importantly, be able to move on and achieve the goals and aspirations I had set for myself. It would not benefit me holding onto this grudge. I felt triumphant and when we left the mediation office, she was quiet, deep in thought. I left her standing outside the mediation office and went back to the office, where I sat at my desk without saying a word to anyone. They all knew where I had been and with whom so, there was no need to say anything; not that I was going to since I realised that I could not trust any of them.

Things were never the same after that day, I think Deidre knew she had overstepped using the mediation as a way to keep me under control. Her little outburst when I addressed what I thought we should have been discussing, was not once mentioned, let alone discussed. I did mention the outcome of the mediation session to Louanne, my husband, sister and my friends. In fact, I told anyone who had witnessed the impact of bullying on my normally cheerful self. Four months later Deidre announced that she was leaving. I was not there at the time, so Louanne filled me in on the news when I returned. My first thoughts were gleeful. I was glad she was going to make someone else's life a complete misery as she had made mine, then I thought that was ugly and I should not wish that treatment on anybody else. It was then that I found out that she was going to another healthcare organisation where she had no line management responsibilities.

At the same time, I was yearning for a job nearer home, as I had been travelling from East to West London for four years, and no matter how early I arrived at the underground station, the platform was always packed. Some mornings I deliberately waited for a couple of trains to pass before I finally got one. Then I decided to drive to work instead and found that when I got in by 7:30am on most days, I completed my work before everyone else arrived or the phones began ringing. Soon, I began looking for work again. I wanted a fresh challenge, for when my son started school. Looking back, and as a woman of Faith, I think the Almighty had other plans for me and needed me to go through those trials and tribulations, to strengthen me for my next job and, also, I would not have had the experiences to share with others and the material to write this book!

Eventually, I got a job close to home where I could literally roll out of bed and into my office as it was so close. I left the organisation and, heard a while later that Deidre knew I was leaving and said to one of my colleagues that she thought I would have stayed, especially since she was no longer there. I, on the otherhand, sincerely hoped she had found happiness wherever she went.

This had been my first healthcare organisation and there were plenty of bullying and harassment incidents that happened while I was there, leading me to believe that bullying and harassment was not only endemic, but was also hidden by those in authority and power. As a Black woman, my eyes were opened to how I consistently needed to prove my worth in more senior roles and it was apparent that the higher I went, the worse it got.

Like the time I had applied for and won a bursary enabling me to study for a post graduate certificate entitled Black Leadership in White Organisations, with the University of East London (UEL). The course was facilitated by two Black psychotherapists who interviewed all the participants before they were allowed to begin. This programme was open to Black and minority ethnic individuals and that in itself caused an uproar. It was while my siblings and I were burying our mother in the Caribbean that I received the news about my successful bursary application. I later found out - from Louanne and Beatrice - that the Associate Director, Deidre's ex-boss had been on the panel. The other panel members had asked her to step down from the judging panel when she had made it clear that she did not want me to get the bursary. Another time the AD, on hearing I was leaving, tried clawing back the money my previous line manager had invested in me before she left. It was amusing to see the great lengths she went to, manipulating the situation in order to exact her revenge against me and stopping me from having any form of development. In addition to the bursary, there were other incidents where I requested development support and was denied by her but being resourceful and self-funded, I did what I needed to do. So, she had not succeeded there either.

When I look back, I likened those experiences to that of a rollercoaster ride. Not just the one but a quite few. Picture yourself at Alton Towers, Disneyland or Disney World, where there was an array of rollercoasters and other rides, evoking a range of emotions from those who ventured onto them. Some rides made you laugh, some made you cry while some made you scream in terror. Now picture me in those working environments, experiencing the same ride, all of these emotions, for all those years.

There were times I thought I would explode or give up because there was no respite from the onslaught of those who consistently abused their role and responsibilities as managers. I remember how I felt when I was pregnant and that was a really trying time for me, but I ensured I would not allow my emotions to affect my son. To be honest, there were times I was convinced he was going to be born traumatised but thank the Almighty we were blessed with a very happy baby boy.

You see, it had not mattered what I did or how I tried to ease the situations, there was always someone ready, willing and able to use their positon and power to enslave, misuse and abuse me. Now, I really empathise with how workers in the many sweat shops around the globe were being mistreated. Do not get me wrong, I was not referring to the Square Mile or City of London to that of a sweat shop but simply mentioning how they must feel being relentlessly mistreated, day-in-day-out. All I would say was thank God for my family, friends and counsellors; yep, I was counselled. Though not mentioned in this book, I went through counselling nonetheless, especially to make sense of what I had been through and to unpack how I felt in order to move on. It was well worth it as I managed to purge the demons I had encountered in the workplace!

At the beginning of this book, I said it was not a *'boo hoo'* look at what others had done to me book but a snapshot of my Journey to Empowerment and the many challenges I met and needed to overcome. Facing these challenges have made me who I am today but it has also given me the confidence to speak up and write about my experiences.

Chapter 12 - A Tripartite of Indifference

"If Moderation is a fault, then
Indifference is a crime."
~ Jack Kerouac ~

Putting Things into Context

When I wrote this chapter, I was flooded with a wave of emotions. This was the hardest part of my journey thus far. It was here, as a senior manager, I experienced the most despicable and, deplorable mistreatment ever. I mean... victimisation, bullying, lying and consistent gatekeeping; all of which was done by my senior manager.

I had left one healthcare organisation and walked right into another healthcare organisation that was going to be merged into a mega healthcare institution. This union was to consist of three large acute hospitals coming together with a total of fifteen thousand staff. I was forewarned by the hiring manager about the potential problems and thought not a problem 'been there, done that' but nothing had prepared me for what actually took place within the four years and seven months I was there.

I was not the only Black person in the team but, again, I was the only Black manager at a senior level, one who was not only a systems trainer but also a HR skills trainer and leadership and development consultant. There were six other Black staff members, four of whom did clinical training and two who were administrative and working in reception. Eventually, I ended working with the clinical trainers after I had revamped the organisation's corporate induction programme. I knew this project would prove to be very challenging, especially with trying to coordinate the imminent changes with the presenters.

Before long I had my first encounter with a very rude presenter, apparently this individual disliked me updating the process or rearranging the order of the sessions. He rang me one day, shouting down the phone: "How dare you change the order of the induction. Who gave you permission?" I handled him very professionally and told him his line manager was the one who had endorsed the changes. I was not to know that this was just a taster of what was to come.

After what I had been through in my first job in the NHS, I never envisaged I would be going through another episode of bullying but by the sixth month, the ugliness of discrimination, bullying and harassment made themselves known. One day, I heard slightly raised and angry voices coming from one of the offices. At first, I was surprised, especially when Agnes and Femi, the two admin members of staff, told me what was happening and I began to see what was exactly happening around me.

I shared my office with Rita - a white woman – who had begun a couple of months before me and line-managed the clinical trainers. Agnes regularly visited our office, dropping off documents and grabbing coffee from the kitchen. Most times Rita would not be around, so she would stay and chat with me. I suppose not being her line manager it was easier for her to talk with me on how she truly felt about work.

One day I asked her about her own development, that was when she said she felt she was being unfairly treated by her line manager. I felt sorry for her especially since she had been at the department's lowest grade for quite a few years. When I enquired if she had been given any opportunity to develop, she said that each time she applied for a programme to upskill herself, it would be denied by her line manager. So, she had been blocked at every angle and given vague reasons as to why she was not entitled to any training. Her line manager had said she would follow up with developmental pointers for her to work on before she even considered signing off any request. Agnes was crestfallen and I realised she was accepting her situation, allowing it to become a way of life. I was certain too that her frequent trips to my office were not going unnoticed. So, I discouraged her from doing so by saying we could talk after work or when no one else was around.

One particular day, Rita had a meeting with one of her junior staff members about some work she was doing. We shared the same office space. At the same time, I was focused on a new presentation I was working on and so happened to have overhead the staff member complaining about the length of time it took for her to create her presentation. Suddenly I heard Rita say, "Don't worry about that, I'll get Jacqueline to tidy it up for you." I was astounded. We were on the same pay grade and, more to the point, she was not my line manager. I looked directly at Rita and said, "What you meant to say was *you'd ask Jacqueline if she has time to help you as she has her own job to do.*" They stared at me, said nothing and just carried on talking as if I was not there. I was extremely angry. When the staff member left, I calmly said to Rita, "Rita, I'm not here to tidy up or create presentations for you or any of your staff. I don't mind giving advice on the best way of producing presentations but I've my own work to do. In addition, we're on the same pay grade. Therefore, you're not my line manager."

Rita stared coldly at me but said nothing. I added I just wanted to make things very clear between us. I learnt a long time ago that I needed to have clear boundaries, and even though I did not mind helping out once in a while, I was not there to be trodden on. *Well, who told me to stand up for myself?* After that day she was very cool towards me, greeting me good morning only if I greeted her first, but I was okay with that since I was always polite. Rita on the other hand, seemed to be watching my every move, listening in on any conversation I had in the office. Between us, we never had any personal conversations and on a regular basis, she would go out for walks with our direct line manager, who was a smoker. I would like to think that was when she reported things about me.

At first, I was not bothered but soon enough it seemed our line manager was listening to Rita, since she started giving me the projects Rita's team were supposed to do. This to me, was the first indication that even though I was a senior manager and equal to Rita, I was being treated like I was her administrator. Eventually, it got a point where I could not stand being in the office when she was present and longed to begin my portfolio of training that way, I would be out most days. That suited me fine since any work they needed to do, they would need to do it themselves. Whenever Rita became stressed, she became very dictatorial, barking orders to her team, telling them to get the work completed, and once it was done, she would suddenly return to her normal, pleasant demeanour. Two sides of a coin.

After our little incident, it was not long before we clashed again. It was inevitable. She was still probably smarting at the way I had corrected her in front of her direct report and one afternoon, while preparing a training programme I was due to run, I printed some documents, stacking them on my desk. As I did so, I started to get frustrated at Rita's mountainous paperwork migrating onto my desk, leaving me with hardly any room. On a couple of occasions, I would ease them back, placing a filing tray or my pen holder as a makeshift barrier. But as they mixed, they caused mine to fall to the floor, dragging my filing tray, my pen pot and anything else I had used as a barrier, with it. I was incensed as I picked them up, restacking them, I was fuming. At that moment Rita reentered the office. I just let rip. I told her in no uncertain terms to keep her documents under control and she needed to get rid of all the paperwork she had piled on top and behind her desk since they were a fire hazard. Well, she did not hold back either and said the paperwork was on her desk and not mine, accusing me of stacking them too high! I said I was not arguing and she should just keep her stuff on her side of the room. Such a contrast of where we sat and whenever people came into our office, they would comment on how untidy her area looked. It took a little while for Rita to realise she was being unreasonable, and I came to understand that before I was hired the office was hers, she was able to spread her stuff. Now that I was there, she needed to move to one side. I likened her behaviour to that of a hoarder. She did not apologise but we called a truce, nonetheless, as we needed to work closely with each other. it made more sense to be cordial with each other and whenever we were in the room together, the temperature between dropped considerably lower.

Mistaking Kindness for Weakness

I was glad I had started training as this was my passion. I did not have much dealings with HR but realised they conducted some induction training and other standalone workshops. One day, my line manager suggested I support one of the HR Business Partners with a one-day programme she facilitated. Sonja (or Sonia) and I met and when she smiled I saw that it never reached her eyes. We talked about the programme and how it was to be delivered; she said she would share information with me, but this never happened. Eventually, I received an email informing me when, where and what time the training would take place. On the day of the training I turned up early but still did not know what I would be doing to support her. When I arrived, she was setting up a laptop, I asked what I was supposed to be doing. It was then that she showed me the paperwork and I realised that she had no intention of letting me deliver on her programme. In fact, it became apparent that she just needed an assistant to hand out the group exercises and other paperwork. It was clear to me what my role on her programme would be.

I was not her or anybody else's lackey, but still I gave her the benefit of the doubt by assisting on another programme. But it happened again. She ran the session while I ran around doing her bidding. She would do the first part and leave me with the "graveyard shift" – collecting the assessments, packing and dropping off the material and equipment to her office. After the second programme I was not going for a hat-trick of being used as it felt like I was being asset-stripped of my qualifications and experience. Well, I had programmes of my own to promote and that was exactly what I did, scheduling the workshops to coincide with her programme. I never said a word to her.

One morning, I got a phone call from one of the HR administrators in Sonja's office, asking if I could cover her programme for the day. I said I could not as I needed to go and do my own training. She said she would inform Sonja. I was irritated with Sonja, she obviously felt that it was unnecessary for her to speak to me in person, feeling it was more fitting to get one of her assistants to ask me if I could cover. Yes, she may have been busy, but I doubted that since changes in the department meant less work was available. Things were changing and with the merger on the horizon, work started to slow down in HR. due to changes with certain roles and the structure of the department. Needless-to-say, I never did any further training with her and my line manager never mentioned anything to me about it either.

Soon, there were talks of a merger and eventually, a series of high-level meetings signed off on a deal. A flurry of meetings, briefings and workshops ensued with everyone needing to participate and contribute; our department was where these sessions were to take place. The merger took place and people flooded into our department for transition programmes, delivered by myself and my colleagues. Part of the merger also meant our training department had grown with two training centres managed by myself and my counterpart, who was from one of the other trusts that had recently merged with us.

The Uphill Struggle

With all what was happening in the organisation, there was bound to be some kind of power-play and struggle across it. The merger should have been transformational but was in fact transactional, where departments were supposed to discuss, agree and sign off on new ways of collaborating and working together in harmony, but this was not happening. Yet, it was not just our department feeling the squeeze, some staff felt and vocalised that the whole process felt more like a takeover than a merger. They felt that they had no voice or choice in what was happening, and it seemed to be driven by the more dominant of the three merging organisations. With all the changes for an integrated programme we had submitted, none were incorporated into the final documentation. It seemed we had gone through the exercise in vain, resulting in the odds being stacked against us.

The whole process was like stepsiblings having to live together, sharing everything from toys to holidays to their parent's time; all of which was always monopolised by the oldest and biggest, bullying their way to the front, time and time again. I was irritated at wasting our time with devising an unused programme, especially since our efforts and time taken to work on it was not even taken into consideration. The radical changes were also causing the spread of rumours of bullying and harassment from staff at all levels. I became extremely busy running stress and change management workshops, plus career coaching sessions for those being made redundant or transitioning into other roles in the newly merged organisation. Everything was difficult to deal with since each person came with their own baggage and it was hard for them to see the bigger picture or any positivity on the horizon. As a result, the majority of staff I coached, felt the organisation had discarded them. I tried supporting them in the best way I could, signposting them to the relevant areas where they could find solace and a possible solution in finding their next job, but it was an uphill struggle, even in our own department. We knew our own department would eventually be pared back since there was duplication across all three organisations. In the end, it would emerge as one single organisation.

It was during this time, I was presented with an opportunity from Lorna, an Associate Director, in our newly created training infrastructure. She rang me, out of the blue, offering me a secondment within her medical education training department which was totally different in practices and procedures to what we were doing within the training department. To be quite honest, I was suspicious because I did not know her and was curious as to why she chose to ask me to take on this role out of a large, amalgamated training team. Nonetheless, I knew nothing about medical education but was intrigued in gaining experience from working with doctors and senior clinicians. She encouraged me to consider a six-month secondment and went on to say that I would be doing them a favour, since the medical education manager on our site needed to move due to the untimely departure of the medical education manager on another site.

I said I would consider it over the weekend and would respond the following week. Come Monday morning, she did not even give me a chance to get my coat off before she rang, pressing me for an answer. I thought about it and decided that I would be learning something new so there was no harm in doing the secondment.

Nothing prepared me for the horrors of working under this woman.

And So It Began...

The first indication that I had made a big mistake was just before I was due to start the secondment. I had booked a series of meetings with Lorna to look at the role and my responsibilities within the six-month period. I took notes, carefully documenting our meetings and was informed that part of the job was to manage a £760k budget; I had never managed a budget of this size before, so I asked for training. I was assured I would get it. Everything was nearly finalised when I had one more meeting with Lorna. I did a handover to another manager who would have been made redundant, so it was an ideal opportunity for her to stay and gain some experience.

On the day of our last meeting, Lorna arrived thirty minutes late and rather flustered. She told me she could not stay long because there was another meeting she needed to attend. So, she proceeded to give me instructions on what she wanted me to do when I began the role. I felt a bit annoyed at her tardiness and the fact that she just launched into giving me instructions without apologising for being late! That was a red flag. I opened my notebook, stopping her before she went into full flow, letting her know that I needed to clarify the points we agreed on in our previous meetings; especially as I was worried about having to manage a large budget without the proper training. She listened and answered each point but when I asked about the budget for training, she paused and matter-of-factly said, "There's no money so you'll just have to sit with the medical education manager you're taking over from for the training." And with that, she promptly said she had to go and left.

I felt like I had been set up, in fact I was sure I had been set up *"like a kipper"* because my line manager was happy to let me go on secondment and even Rita seemed a lot more cheerful towards me. I was angry and when I got home, I carefully constructed an email to Lorna outlining my concerns at some of the things that had arisen during the course of our conversations. I concluded that I felt I had been duped into accepting a role where I was more than likely to fail because there was no adequate support for me while learning on the job. Being from the corporate world I was taught to be transparent so, I copied her line manager and the executive director into the email. What I had not realised, was that what I had referred to as transparency, was deemed to be whistleblowing in the NHS and this was not taken lightly in the healthcare environment... as I was about to find out.

Hell Hath No Fury

Well, imagine the backlash I received from Lorna after she was called into her boss's office to explain herself the following Monday morning. I was at a half-day team briefing. The meeting was to take place at 9:30am and at 9:45am everybody was asking for her, everyone except me. I knew exactly where she was but said nothing. Finally, when she did arrive, it was nearly lunch time and the team were talking among themselves. As she walked in, the look on her face said it all. She was very unhappy. The managers and Tracey - Lorna's assistant - took their leave while I stayed since I had my pack lunch with me.

When everyone was gone Lorna launched into an angry but controlled tirade on how insubordinate I had been for sending the email and copying everyone into it. She said that I should have come to her with my concerns. I pointed out to her, that I had in fact spoken to her about my concerns, but her response was not what we had agreed on in our meetings. I said I was being set up to fail. She became angry, storming out of the room. I was uncertain as to where she went and just ate my lunch. After a while the other managers and Tracey returned, asking what had happened as to why Lorna was so late, I said I did not know and left it at that. What happened as a result of this one act became a catalogue of Lorna's ineptitude around protocol, policies and procedures, and the lengths that individuals would go in gate-keeping information, keeping it behind closed doors. Over a period of time Lorna's incessant and unrelenting bullying, victimisation and lying took my stress levels to a whole different level, one I had never experienced before.

Lorna was a tall and sturdy in stature and though she seemed pleasant, I saw through her façade to who she really was. I also observed her mistreatment of others. When mergers or changes occurs within an organisation, staff tended to be promoted to more senior levels and, more often than not, with little or no experience in managing the role. Lorna was a classic example. During the merger another more suitable manager had missed the job posting and the closing date, so, it became a one-horserace. Before the merger, Lorna had started at the same level as me and the other education managers but by whatever means, she ended up triple jumping into the position she now held.

As I mentioned before, when individuals got into these positions without training, their biases would 'kick in' and, they tended to use their position and power to shutdown, suppress or bully other individuals into submission. This is more often due to their lack of people and performance management skills, inadequate professional development or leadership training.

It did not take Lorna long to start finding fault in my work. Apparently, it seemed she had been sharpening her claws on Tracey - her Black assistant. It affected poor Tracey so much that she seemed to have lost all of her confidence and began to work later and later, trying to ensure that her work was perfect for Lorna, who would even go as far as ask her to redo any work she had just completed. Even though I had not been in the department for long, it felt like Lorna was not finished with me and I felt as if I was waiting for *'Madame Guillotine'* to drop her deadly blade.

I was tasked along with the other medical education managers to produce a project plan for a new department structure; each of us working on segments. Every time I completed and submitted my document, it was thrown back at me with a note from Lorna saying that it was wrong and not what she had asked for. This scenario happened to one other manager – Sangita, an Asian woman. And although we had weekly meetings with Lorna, we could not fathom what she really wanted. But a third medical education manager, Sharon - a white woman - did not seem to have any problems with her submitted work and whenever we were in her presence, Sangita and I would not air how we felt about Lorna, just in case she went back and told her.

This was a sad existence, especially for us.

One day, I was off work and decided to speak to Lorna's boss to let her know how I was being treated. I felt that her boss should be made aware of how Lorna was treating her staff. I was unsure what I wanted her to do but felt I needed to let someone higher up know how this woman was behaving towards me and the affect it was having on my work. We spoke for about thirty minutes and afterwards, I was relieved that I had spoken to someone in authority. Someone who could do something about this abusive behaviour. How wrong was I.

My call only made matters worse in my already diminished relationship with Lorna. It was obvious that her boss had spoken with her because she made a point of letting me know that a conversation had taken place between her and her boss about me! It seemed my conversation was for nothing. Lorna could spin a good and convincing story and that was exactly what she had done, she always made out that I failed to grasp and understand the role properly, not knowing what I was doing. This was nothing short of a red card on a football field. But Lorna was good, nothing was obvious, and she chose her moments very carefully whenever she was about to bully me, ensuring no witnesses were around when she did.

She came to my office a few days after the phone call with her boss. I just left my office and turned a corner in the corridor and came face-to-face with her. She caught me off-guard in a blind spot, where no one was, the area was deserted. She towered over me as on that particular day, I was wearing flat shoes. I felt small standing in front of her. Sneering, she said, "Don't you ever go speaking to my boss about me again." I was surprised as well as distraught and quickly sidestepping by her, I hastily returned to my office. I was not used to that type of aggressive behaviour and I immediately went to my computer, composed and sent an email to her line manager, informing her of what had just happened.

While I was having my baptism of fire with Lorna, so was Tracey and things were only getting from bad to worse until, one day, she completely lost it. She lashed back at Lorna's persistence in rubbishing her work and telling her she was not doing a good job. She just snapped. Later, she sent emails to various individuals telling them of what Lorna had been doing, exposing the vile behaviour that this woman had subjected her to. Both Sangita and I received an email informing us that Lorna was secretly going to HR, trying to performance manage us without our knowledge. With my master's degree in Human Resource Management, I instinctively knew that what Lorna was doing was wrong and not in line with policies or procedures. So, I had nothing to lose and forwarded the email to her boss highlighting my own experience with Lorna, telling her I was not impressed with what she was doing. By the time I received Tracey's email, she had been released from her job and unceremoniously expelled from the organisation without anyone getting a chance to speak with her. I later learnt that Tracey had spoken to Lorna's line manager, just as I had done; telling her about the mistreatment she was facing under her management but this fell on deaf ears and since Tracey was a contract member of staff this made it easier to get rid of her without her voice being heard or her claims being fairly investigated and dealt with.

Imagine the hell that broke loose when this hit the organisation's newsstand. By then, I was not sleeping well at nights and the fatigue began to show. I was getting so weary and stressed out by just jumping through the hoops that Lorna kept placing in front of me. I was getting extremely fed up with the gatekeeping that was going in the department, since nothing was being done about her behaviour. I felt as if I was being left for her to deal with me harshly every time I complained to her boss or even her bosses' boss. Even though my complaint went straight to the board; alas, nothing was done and to be honest, all it did was place a bullseye on my back.

One evening I was at home talking to my husband and daughter about what was going on at work, when all of a sudden and without warning, I puked all over the floor. I was as frightened as they were and with a searing pain in my head I was rushed upstairs to lie down. My husband called the doctor's surgery and I had an emergency appointment that evening. As I sat in the doctor's waiting room, I felt the tears fighting to breakthrough but held them back until the he called me in. Before I even sat, the floodgates immediately opened, and I started sobbing uncontrollably. The poor doctor did not know what to say but offered me a box of tissues while patiently waiting until I had stopped. I felt bad yet safe at the same time. So, I told him what had been happening to me at work and as I did, he took my blood pressure. When he did the reading, there was a look of concern on his face, so he took another three. My blood pressure was sky high. He signed me off from work and said I needed to go home and rest.

I was off for a month and even though I was out of the office and on sick leave, Lorna still tried to bully me via emails. The way in which she wrote them I could actually hear her voice in my head. It was all too much for me and I decided that upon my return to work, I was going to terminate my secondment and return to my previous role. This did not go down well with Lorna or my previous line manager, since many changes had occurred while I was on secondment. From what I heard, Rita had our office all to herself once again and it looked like she was not going to share it with me or anyone else any time soon. I decided I would move into an empty office located next door.

Even though I was back in my old role Lorna's bullying and undermining still reached me. When I returned to my previous role, no one and I meant absolutely no one, wanted to be seen talking to me, least they too were caught up in the drama. Believe me, I was working in an organisation of 15,000 people and I never felt so isolated or alone. I then decided I would submit a grievance against Lorna and thank goodness for my intimate knowledge as a trainer, where I taught about bullying, harassment and effective documentation in safeguarding oneself; I was able to compile my evidence. It was really a case of *physician heal thyself*, because all of the training I had disseminated to others, I was now using for myself.

I had designed a simple yet effective template to capture the information and by using my meeting notes I was able to type up clear and concise incidents that had occurred. As I began to compile the document, I recalled the tasks I had been given, realising that some were unachievable. Funnily, some were similar to what her own line manager had given her to do as a part of *her* job. I was so glad I had terminated my secondment, because had I not, my line manager, Lorna and HR would have forced me to stay in that role. All I could do was thank the Almighty. *Imagine what it would have been like had I stayed?* Anyway, I was tucked away in my office with only my iPad, playing my favourite gospel, rare groove, R&B and reggae compilations; to keep me company and my spirits buoyed as I typed. As I mentioned before, when one was on this journey, it was a lonely road to travel, since nobody wanted to travel on the road with you, no matter how friendly they were with you beforehand; they would steer clear as if you carried the plague. That was exactly what was happening with me. After all, I wore a bullseye.

This was sad, because while I was going through my trials and tribulations with Lorna, I was receiving phone calls from members of staff who needed my support, as they too were being bullied by their own line managers. So, pushing my own feelings aside, I helped them document their incidents and signposted them to where they needed to go, like occupational health. One day, I got a phone call from a HR manager asking if I would coach someone who they deemed was aggressive. I said I would but whatever was discussed, was done in total confidence and I was not obliged to tell them anything.

The individual visited me for his coaching session. He was a white male doctor and I was surprised that there was no one else who could have coached him. He was a consultant and burly man of 6ft 5inches, and I was like a midget next to him. But it only took me a short time to realise that he was not aggressive at all, because he too had been severely bullied in a previous healthcare organisation he had worked at. For him, it was a case of fight or flight, so he took flight and came to our organisation expecting some respite. What he got was staff shortages, lack of service provision and little empathy from the higher echelons and with all these things stacked against him, he was unstable. The unresolved issues around bullying and harassment added to him being primed to burst; which was exactly what had happened, he had a mini meltdown in the hospital and HR's interpretation of him was that he was been aggressive!

I empathised with him because I could relate but could not imagine being in his shoes, in his position, as a doctor within the hospital with no support at all. So, I listened, even offering him tea and biscuits. After he told me his story, I shared with him some tips on how he could alleviate his stress and it was six weeks later that I heard from him and glad he to hear he was working out his stress. He said that he was sleeping much better after implementing some of the tips I gave him. I wished him well on his road to recovery. He also thanked me for listening to him.

By this time, I had completed my own grievance paperwork and was ready to submit it to HR. The indifference I felt all around me was cloying and, no matter where I turned, it was already seated at the table mingling with my work colleagues. My paperwork totaled ninety-one pages and as I wrote the number down, I was surprised that over a five-month period so many incidents had occurred, showing Lorna's pattern of behaviour and micro-aggressions. I persisted for another six weeks before anyone within HR acknowledged receipt of my grievance or started an investigation. When they finally responded, they sent a letter explaining that a senior staff member would do an investigation. I rejected this, citing that they were all from the same directorate and I would not get a fair hearing or outcome. So, an external investigator was found - a Black woman. From what I knew, when an investigation was being conducted the investigator was supposed to interview the victim first and not the perpetrator. Well, that never happened in my case. I was fine with the fact that they had chosen a Black investigator and in the back of my mind, wondered if this would make any difference since all the policies and protocols had already been breached in the process. The investigation was not going to start following protocol now, especially as the investigator agreed to interview the bully first. Another big red flag and let down in my eyes. Thus, I was not expecting anything different with the outcome.

I met with the investigator and told her my side of the story but as I suspected, she had been *'knobbled'*, stepping outside of her duty of care as an investigator to get the facts and be impartial in the process. I came away deflated. The investigator's questions seemed quite closed as if she was using a script to elicit the relevant information from me to help the perpetrator. Later, I heard that Lorna had been well known for her bullying tactics with staff even before the merger and her subsequent appointment to the role;

everyone knew but nobody dared go against her. I felt ill to know that the organisation's leaders knew full well that some of their managers were serial abusers and had done nothing about it. Only moving the person on or, in most cases, getting rid of the victim in some way or another.

It was around about this time, that I got introduced to Roger Kline, a research Fellow at Middlesex University and author of the report: *'Snowy White Peaks of the NHS'*, (if you have not read it, I suggest you do so) which lifted the lid on discrimination within governance and leadership, and the potential impact on patient care in London and England. It was such a huge relief. Just having a talk with someone who saw things from my perspective and knew all too well about the reality of what severe and persistent bullying could do to a person's mindset, character, emotions, skills and performance. I was so thankful to Roger for taking the time to listen to me, giving me sound and grounding advice that helped me to overcome the adverse situation I found myself in.

When the investigation was finally concluded, I heard nothing from HR or my department for quite a while but, nonetheless, I pressed them for answers and in my pursuit for justice. I happened to catch one of the HR managers off guard and asked her outright, what had happened to my case and found that my grievance had actually been upheld 100% but no one had even bothered to inform me. I decided I needed to take the initiative. So, on one occasion, I asked for a copy of the redacted report but, each time I asked, the answer I was the same, "it would not serve me any purpose", but I persisted. Eventually, I received it and after I printed the first page, I raised it to the light and saw the redacted text. I was able to read every word Lorna had said to the investigator and - lo and behold - her very first sentence started out with a lie. Now that I knew my grievance had been upheld, it was time to see how and when the disciplinary proceedings would take place. In a lot of cases where Black people had been victimised and bullied by a white senior member of staff, the victim somehow turned into the perpetrator while the "real" perpetrator was either moved into another job or left the organisation before any justice could be meted out.

While I waited for the outcome, I was contacted by a recruitment consultant based in the Middle East with an offer of a role in a private women's and children's hospital in Qatar. I was being headhunted! I was intrigued and explored my options, including consulting with my family if I should accept. They said I should, and I applied. My first interview was a presentation over Skype in front of a panel consisting of the HR recruiter, Learning and Development manager, the Director for National Development and a Trainer.

While awaiting their decision, new revelations came to light at work and I guess with all that had been happening with Lorna and the grievance, a restructure within the directorate needed to happen. I had mentioned that the victim somehow would turn into the perpetrator and their position terminated, this was a classic example of the rules being bent to get the outcome they wanted. Unbeknownst to me, my return had caused a tsunami in the department, especially since I had terminated the secondment. If I had stayed the entire term of the secondment, they would have made it a permanent role, and I could have done nothing about it. Needless to say, my counterpart was very cool towards me since she was currently heading the department, so there was no way she could have line managed me. If she did, then I would be forced to leave and, that could have been deemed grounds for constructive dismissal, and that was something they did not want to have to deal with alongside my grievance.

Although I had done everything within the policies and procedures, they still wanted me to leave the organisation. Out of the blue I was being contacted by recruitment agents who I had never heard of or signed with. They sent me emails or tried connecting with me via LinkedIn asking me for an up-to-date resume. Anyway, I was not fooled and started my own investigation. One recruiter was so familiar with me that it made me suspicious, so I looked her up on LinkedIn and who she was connected with and found that she was linked to Lorna's line manager! That was not just a coincidence.

Still, I played the game and went through with the organisation's restructure and interview process, knowing full well that the end result would be my failure in attaining the job. I felt that they already had the person they wanted and naturally, the process had looked above-board thus no one could question their ethics around it. In fact, that the interviewer was the line manager of my counterpart before the merger! Coincidence? I think not.

My plan was to leave the organisation, but I wanted them to make me redundant, especially as I knew they wanted me to leave without anything. Come on... I was not going to leave my nine-plus years' of working within the National Health Service. Having had to deal with this abhorrent behaviour and mistreatment, as well as having to deal with persons who knew exactly what they were doing, being totally conscious of their actions and the effect it had on others.

The interview date was set, and I attended, said all the right things and went through the motions. When it came to receiving feedback and being told I was unsuccessful, I think the manager was taken aback at how calm I responded. I was not mad nor was I going to let them stereotype me, since that was the excuse others needed to justify their behaviour meted out to Black people. I thanked her, asking for the interview notes. So, there I was, being made redundant again.

The HR Manager who was dealing with my redundancy had taken it upon herself to inform me that I would not be receiving my redundancy payout for at least two months after my last day in the organisation. When I asked why, she merely said that these things happened. Well, I knew that was untrue, so when I received my final pay and saw only half of my normal salary, I decided to take matters into my own hands. I emailed the HR Director to clarify the situation.

It was my right to do so and I felt that this HR Manager had no grounds to withhold my redundancy payment without there being a proper reason behind it. She was being spiteful and vindictive. Yet, this was the same HR Manager (who happened to be Black) who had dealt with my grievance. It was bad enough being vilified by the white people I worked with but to have the same treatment meted out by a fellow Black woman, I felt sorry and ashamed for her. The HR Director responded to my email very quickly, confirming what I suspected all along. I was being treated unfairly.

I received my redundancy on the due date and exactly four weeks after I had left the organisation. I was ready to fly out to Qatar for a new adventure.

My time in the NHS, the largest healthcare organisation in UK and probably Europe, was fraught with good, bad and a whole heap of indifference. I was not bitter, but I was deeply saddened, because the NHS seemingly failed to encourage or support Black people in senior positions, consistently moved the goalposts to ensure rising and aspiring Black leaders never actually got appointed into those positions of seniority and power. I do not know why but think about it, there were so many Black people ready to step into senior positions yet what was really happening was that they were encouraged to do more managerial training, sometimes taking them out of the running for any position for up two years. In effect, halting their progression as they were being "developed". To me, it was like putting them onto a conveyor belt, like in airport baggage claims and if you missed your luggage, you had to wait until it came around again. This was what was happening to Black members of staff.

I learnt a lot during my time there. I learnt to *sing whilst in the valley*. A term I used when a friend once asked me that with everything I had been through, why was I still optimistic and happy. I said I knew where I was coming from, where I was going and had faith in the one who stopped me from falling. I learnt to sing because that was what kept me calm, enabling me to be available and in a position to help others going through the same challenges I had faced.

You see, it had not mattered where I went in the organisation, the result would be the same. Nevertheless, whatever was going on or how I felt, I knew I would be the best I could be in order to support, train, coach and develop others. After all, I was not the only one who was severely bullied, others were going through it and some still were.

Knowing this, how could I stay and be consistently asset-stripped by an organisation that clearly was and still is unwilling to really deal with the endemic bullying and harassment that lay deeply entrenched within.

Chapter 13 - Full of Eastern Promise

"Release: As soon as I change my focus and,
Let go of what no longer serves my highest good,
I create space for greater fulfilment in my life."
~ Healing Light Online ~

The Healing Balm

I was victorious having successfully had my grievance upheld and justice served on the perpetrator; yet somehow, I felt broken, battered and bruised. I never envisaged my life within what was purported to be the 'caring profession', to render me to that of a green army recruit. The hospital's ethos being that more like the military. As I left this battlefield, I felt that this new venture and experience in the Middle East would give me some respite and the thought of leaving my family behind in the UK, although heart-wrenching, was indeed what I needed to do. I was fractured in ways I could not even describe and if I stayed, one of three things would have happened – I could have ended up in jail, with mental health problems or dead due to an aneurism exploding in my head brought on by high blood pressure and the severe stress I had endured. So, I needed to find solace somewhere else and this opportunity in a far-off land, in a new role, seemed filled with promise, novelty and an introduction into a different culture. A place where I could start applying the healing balm to a consistently open wound that quite frankly, never had a chance to properly heal over the years I had been working.

All those places, knowledge and skills were emblazoned on my resume but never truly told the stories of the persistent bullying, harassment, victimisation, exclusion and discrimination. I felt that the Middle East would be a place where I would now have the time and space to put things into perspective, to learn to truly forgive those who had treated me so disparagingly so that I could finally move on with my life, and in doing so, release the blockages that held me back for so long. I felt being away from the UK would help me heal and this was what I needed right there and then.

Even though I had forgiven those who had mistreated me, and moved on to pastures new, a little residue was always left and my Journey to Empowerment was not quite complete. And although I was away from all that ailed me in the UK unbeknownst to me, there was another kind of challenge awaiting me in the Middle East.

Expats Are Us

I landed in Qatar in mid-February, with a couple of suitcases and no expectations.

I had a couple of days' grace before I started my job, so I explored my neighbourhood, finding my feet around The Saray Apartment Hotel - my new home. When I arrived at Doha International Airport, I was given the VIP treatment and fast-tracked through immigration with everything being taken care. All I needed to do was wait and nibble on the beautiful fruit and other delights. My driver – yes, I had a car - took me directly to my accommodation where I checked in. My apartment was absolutely luxurious, not that I lived in an apartment in a foreign country before but it was a two-bed, fully furnished with all mod-cons and a plasma television in every room. I was elated. It felt like I was in London again, living on my own, those many moons ago.

I attended a two-day induction and as part of it we visited the Fanar Qatar Islamic Cultural Center and Museum. All the women in the group donned traditional dress, *abaya* and *hijab*, to cover our heads - especially if we wished to enter the mosque. It was a wonderful experience and an opportunity to learn about Islam and the Qatari culture.

My first day in the office was very interesting, I was collected from reception then passed to my new line manager - Ameena, the director. I was introduced to a few individuals, one of whom was Graham - a manager - and Australian; he was the one who had interviewed me via Skype. He went on to say that I was poached from him. I smiled and said nothing. There was a story behind his comment which was told to me three months later. I was also introduced to the team who were all Qatari nationals bar my counterpart Omar, who was Egyptian. They all gave me a very warm welcome and I was looking forward to the job and especially working with young Qatari graduates.

Before long, I was having my probationary meeting with Ameena. Needless-to-say, I passed with distinction and was humbled by her glowing feedback. At one point, she asked if I remembered anything about my first interview; I said I remembered her entering the interview a little later after it had started. She told me that in the interview, she had been told that they would not be offering the job to me and she could not understand why. So, at the end of the interview, she had probed, asking me additional questions. Then there was the informal chat between her and the Head of HR. It had been strange at the time but listening to her it all made more sense. As had Graham's comment. I was grateful I had found out after I had passed my probation. Imagine Graham's awkwardness if I had responded to his comment, I probably would have said: "It was fair game after all you weren't going to offer me the role!"

My problems began after I passed my probation. At first it was just the little comments. My line manager gave me projects to undertake, equal to that of the other managers. There was one particular occasion, where Graham started really showing how he felt about me and my work. One afternoon, he came, challenging me about a document I had produced. In the document I stated that the manager needed to be in a position to mentor the graduates. He said loudly that he disagreed with what I had written and that: "The manager cannot possibly be a mentor." His voice carried throughout the open-plan office, everyone could hear him.

I calmly responded, "The manager has to be the mentor."

He repeated, "The manager cannot be a mentor Jacqueline."

At this point it felt as if everyone had stopped what they were doing and watched us. I disagreed with him, pointing out where the organisation was at that moment. I said, "The hospital wasn't open for business as yet and the services weren't fully equipped with the staff they needed. Within a typical department you'd find a director, manager and coordinator. You were just assigned with a graduate associate - so who's the mentor? It can't be the director as he was too senior and busy or the coordinator as they were too junior, so, it needed to be the manager."

He continued to disagree with me. I said we would have to agree to disagree. He stormed off without saying another word and over the coming weeks, I was persona non grata as his staff, who had previously been friendly, began to ignore me. But that was not my problem I had no problem with any of them or with their manager. As far as I was concerned we only had a disagreement, nothing more, nothing less.

It was about that time I felt the need to write about how I felt. So, I started writing posts on LinkedIn, my first one inspired by a quote which a friend had sent me. The second, inspired by me successfully passing my probation and entitled: 'As

One Door Closes'. The outpouring through words was so cathartic, a bit like writing this book! My third post was based on the behaviour of staff working for Graham and their friends in different departments. It was amazing the behaviour of these individuals who did not know me but acted as if I had offended them in some way. My third article was entitled: *'When You Look in The Mirror What Do You See?'* and spoke of bullying by association. It was a term I used whenever someone systematically drip-fed poison to others who may or may not know the individual in question but would automatically start acting strangely towards them. These friends would fail to find out anything further, only listening to the person they trusted, even if they were blatantly lying; like a flock of starlings flying in formation as soon as one changed course, the rest followed.

Knowing about Graham's thoughts from the interview process it came as no surprise he had behaved in that way. To make matters worse I was now tasked to do work aligned with some of his projects. Even so, I was not offended by his behaviour because I had already survived two years of this type of behaviour back in the UK. Since a mix of cultures existed in the office, this brought a particular synergy, mindset and behaviour despite where the staff originated from. And for me, I was not going to behave indifferently towards any of them, saying my good mornings or byes as I normally would. Some responded while others completely ignored me. I was not deterred or offended and usually listened to my music on my iPad, to the annoyance of others. A few would comment that I was not even listening to them. I would then take out my earphones and ask whether they wanted to speak with me and, more often than not, they wanted nothing; they were just annoyed since I was ignoring everything that was going on around me. As far as I was concerned, I had work to do.

After my run-in with Graham, nothing further of any significance happened and as the months went by, so my knowledge and experience grew. So much was happening within the organisation for me to worry about rather than what others were saying or doing. But in less than a year, the rumour mills started churning about redundancies. This continued for a bit, then the emails started coming and all of sudden it became official - the organisation needed to shed staff. This meant non-clinical staff would be under scrutiny - someone like me.

One morning Ameena called me and two other senior staff members into a meeting. She informed us of the imminent changes and redundancies, at this point I thanked her for the opportunity to work with her and the team and said if it was my time to go, I would just accept. I was ready to return home since I was missing my family, even though I regularly flew back and forth, it was just not enough.

Eventually, I was one of the staff members being made redundant. Some would say it was unfortunate, but I saw it as being a fantastic opportunity to have shared my knowledge, learned and grow in another country. Gaining such an experience was priceless. So, exactly one year and one month to the day I started in the Middle East, I was making my way back to the UK and to my family. Prior to returning, I had thought long and hard about what I was going to do - would I return to the NHS or would I look for another job? But, the thought of returning to the hamster wheel was not an option for me.

I agonised over this and decided that I could not go back to working fulltime especially with my son now in after-school care. The thought of having to rush to collect him each day, wading through rush-hour traffic was not what I wanted. So, before I landed in the UK, I made the biggest decision in my life - I decided to start my own business. There were many reasons for this independence, I knew the road would not be an easy one and that there would be others out there with the same goals and aspirations as well as expertise. But there was one big difference though, they would not be doing it like me and on that note, I was going to go for it.

During my time in the Middle East not only had I learnt about the culture and the people I also learnt that no matter where you were in the world, bad behaviour and closed mindsets were also there. Someone asked me what it was like being a Black woman working in the Middle East; they also asked if I found the Arabs to be racist. I said that it was not the Arabs I had a problem with, it was everyone else! Being in an organisation with a diverse workforce and mixture of people, there was bound to be some form of disharmony, bullying or even racism.

It was not long after I had joined the organisation that a young African woman, who was a sonographer, and I became friends. We even lived in the same apartment hotel and caught the same bus to work. One day she confided in me that she was being bullied and had nobody to turn to.

She was being bullied so severely by her white colleagues that she could not bear to do the six months in and would resign. They had made her life so unbearable, finding it untenable to stay, she just wanted it to end, especially since she was there on her own. She said it was like being in a lion's den.

I had my own challenges and not everyone had the same level of resilience to tough out certain situations and clearly, she could not stand it any longer. For me, I had decided I was not going to let anyone try and run me out of a role and, whenever I chose to leave, it would be my decision and on my terms. This aside I thoroughly enjoyed my time in the Middle East despite the ups and downs. I was then and still grateful for the opportunities and the journey I had taken since they have brought me to a point where I was now taking a 'leap of faith' and leaving the next chapter of my story to **'Our Maker of Days'** and the one who stopped me from falling. Knowing where He was leading me, would be for my edification, growth and ultimately onto the next chapter of my incredible Journey to Empowerment.

"I was bruised but now I'm healed,
I cried but now my eyes are dry,
my heart was broken and my mind shattered;
a broken and forlorn individual who,
at the lowest point in her life, looked to the highest
for His mercy and grace.
A balm of healing, a soothing touch and rest for a weary and
broken soul; the care and attention made way for restoration and
oh how my heart now sings with joy and constant praise."

Jacqueline A. Hinds © 2018

My Journey to Empowerment

"It is good to have an end to journey toward;
but it is the journey that matters, in the end"
~ Ernest Hemingway ~

To understand my journey, one needs to understand the context of the places I have been and, how my induction into *emotional intelligence* has always been the foundation stone and key feature in shaping of where I have been. More importantly, it has contributed to who I am and, where I currently am today. It also, gives you a little glimpse of where I'm heading…

Some of you may or may not have heard of the term **Emotional Intelligence**. If I was to mention, Daniel Goleman, then you would probably think…oh yes, I have heard of him.   Well, Emotional Intelligence was first introduced by Wayne Payne in 1985. Well, Daniel Goleman is one of a long line of theorists, psychologists and strategists, who have created, shaped and perfected the varied models and theories on emotional intelligence we see and tap into today. I realised very early on and use as a tagline: *"Emotional Intelligence is in Everything We Do"*. Once you realise that it could be tapped into, it could then be used to change the hearts and minds of individuals who really wanted to embrace its concepts; weaving it into their business acumen, skills, social settings and everyday lives.

Emotional Intelligence... What was it?

Emotional Intelligence (EI) was a set of emotional and social skills that collectively establish how well we:

✓ Perceive and express ourselves;

✓ Develop and maintain social relationships;

✓ Cope with challenges;

✓ Use emotional information in an effective and meaningful way.

Basically, it was a predictor for life.

Here were a couple of shorter definitions which were just as useful to use, as quoted by Dr. Hank Clemons in his book *"EQ is for Everyone".*

"Emotional Intelligence is being smart about your emotions"

"Emotional Intelligence is having your emotions work for you rather than against you"

"Emotional Intelligence is the skill and ability to recognise, understand and use emotions effectively"

You see, all along my career journey, I had been using emotional intelligence throughout the various job roles I undertook. It came naturally to me, and as I progressed up the career ladder within a variety of leadership positions; and being able to work within learning and development environments has also helped me immensely in nurturing and growing my EI skills.

I refer to myself as the #EISavvy Coach firstly, because I can and secondly, because I have been working with people ever since I left school at the tender age of 16 and, have developed a skill to connect with people from all walks of life, at whatever level they were at, in order to be able to provide the listening ear, support or development they needed at that juncture.

The pictorial representation highlights and walks you through the incredible journey I have had thus far, and more importantly, it outlines the chapters as a roadmap and timeline of this book.

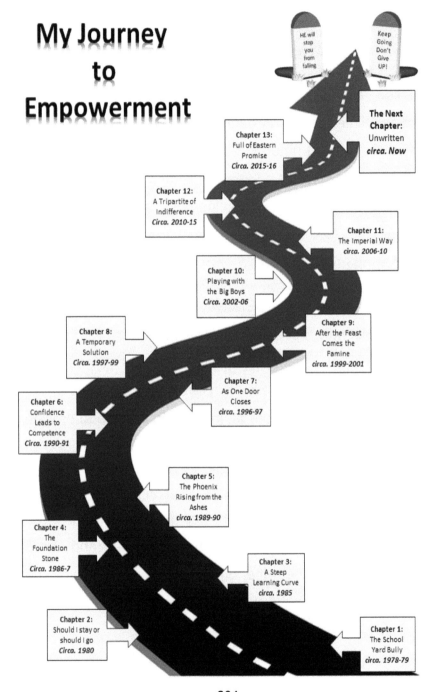

From a Thought Leaders' Perspective

"There's nothing more toxic and demoralizing
than having to work in an environment where
a bully or stealth harasser gets to threaten,
haze, feast, overpower and exist daily."
~ Ty Howard ~

"...I have worked in various senior level roles and, what I have found to be true, that is some leaders manage their staff by creating a fearful culture. Some have used intimidation and bullying in such a way to cause employees so much distress that they become ill with stress and need to seek help from mental health professionals. An example of this... I knew a CEO that was a bully. He terrorised his staff and put unrealistic demands on them. He also flaunted employment law never using the right process to get things done. The business suffered, people left and eventually the company crumbled. It concerns me that organisations do not put enough emphasis in tackling bulling and only consider it a problem when someone points out the financial losses that could occur if not dealt with. What does this show? It shows no real desire to care and support the employees, neither a real desire to ensure policies and procedures are robust enough to deal with those who commit such acts that cause

stress and hurt. The bottom line should be focused on individuals and not finance, which is an indictment of organisations today. Bullying does not cultivate good business practices or ethics, neither does it support employee emotional health and well-being..."

Dianne Greyson, Director Equilibrium Mediation Consulting, HRM Expert, Author (Business Culture Review), Founder of the #EthnicityPayGap movement.

As a BME employee, there were situations and circumstances in my career within corporate positions, where I was subjected to forms of discrimination but, at the time, I did not perceive it to be like that and felt I just had to work and try harder. After an interview, the feedback given was "'you were pipped to the post!" My white counterparts were all appointed in positions above me, even though I was qualified and was more experienced than they were. Another incident springs to mind where, after being shortlisted for several District Nursing roles and, after the interview, being told that "you interviewed well, however your face would not fit in around here". Bullying and harassment has no place within corporate, public or social sector settings and needs to be challenged and eradicated. With the many challenges that were set before me, it brought out a resilience, determination and perseverance of not to give up but to continue to pursue my dream to become a Nurse Consultant. **Shirley A Powell, Founder & Director, Your Life in Your Hands**

"...Few employers need be reminded of the economic costs, some unquantifiable, e.g. boycotting businesses known to have unsavoury business practices, when harassment, bullying, victimisation, discrimination, is permitted to flourish and become institutionalised. It should never be forgotten that those responsible for probity and standards are failing in their statutory duties when refusing to recognise and ethically address unlawful behaviours in the workplace. Also not to be forgotten is that the costs to victims of harassment and discrimination are unacceptably high by any standard Employers who choose to ignore the pain and suffering of targets, including where their behaviour has contributed to driving an employee to suicide, is a strong indicator they have a stubborn disregard towards human rights and compliance. Rather than risk exposure for their culpability, *such employers attempt to silence and cover up, rather than robustly address any potentially unlawful actions. It is shameful albeit all too common that such 'leaders' responsible for failure on what should be a criminal scale, can be richly rewarded for their negligence and irresponsibility. Notwithstanding, Black Lives Matter and #MeToo are proving effective at keeping past offenders in the limelight, and hopefully giving current bullies and abusers of due process, many anxious moments. These campaigns show that anyone being bullied and treated unfairly is not alone. They serve as a reminder that there is no need to stay quiet and acquiesce to unfair treatment, that there is a rich source of talented, morally responsible personnel willing to provide professional, empathetic, expert advice and support..."* **Christine Yates, Director, E&Q Consultancy Ltd**

An issue that doesn't get enough attention is a culture of everyday harassment in the workplace that corrosively saps the will of sections of the workforce and undermines motivation for change. Whether this is continual sexualised banter and innuendo, negative stereotyping of particular sexual orientations or genders or the marginalising of Black, Asian and minority staff's voice and contribution. It acts as a dead weight on the organisation that effectively privileges some staff at the expense of others and undermines confidence of those it stops from being able to be themselves at work, which means they do not get to develop their confidence or feel encouraged to raise their ambitions. Anyone who questions this privileging, particularly a new manager, then gets portrayed as being humourless, politically correct and pandering to marginal groups. Actually, what you need to be doing is being bold in setting out your vision of a vibrant inclusive 21st century workplace that treats its staff as valued individuals and is supported in carrying this into daily behaviour and actions. Too often even when local managers try to do this, they do not get supported by the organisation's senior management and this cements in the feeling of impotence about creating a better working environment. **David Truswell, Executive Director, Dementia Alliance for Culture and Ethnicity & Healthcare Consultant**

"...In my role as Professional Officer for Diversity at the Department of Health between 2009 - 2011 and then as Chair of the Chief Nursing Officer's for England's Black and Minority Ethnic Strategic Advisory Group until March 2017, I have heard and continue to hear, many distressing stories of BME staff being discriminated against, harassed and bullied in the NHS. I have seen the effects of discriminatory behaviour on staff morale, confidence and their mental health and wellbeing. If accountability was enforced on how managers, employers and even colleagues have treated BME staff, then the problem would not be consistently increasing but would be decreasing within the NHS. I remember a Band 6 nurse relying how she had consistently applied for 10 years for promotion to Band 7 in the organisation that she trained in. She was good enough to act up into position but was never successful at interview to get the role. However, the nurses she had mentored as students and supported were successful in moving up the ladder and getting the promotion. Often, she was asked to support and train the person promoted over her, although she had a wealth of experience and knowledge and could do the job. This kind of insidious behaviour is really demoralizing and degrading. The Band 6 nurse has now given up trying and

has resigned herself to the fact that she would not be promoted in the organisation where she trained and has worked for many years. Another BME Nurse at another NHS Trust was never good enough to go to next level but was always called upon to do projects to turn around difficult ward areas and was often recommended for acting up roles but was never successful in getting the promotion. When she left that Trust she secured a senior post very easily. That's why I always say go where you are celebrated and appreciated and do not stay where you are denigrated or tolerated..."
Joan Myers OBE, Associate Director for Health Services and Chief Nurse - Achieving for Children

Workplace bullying, the silent epidemic: *I vividly remember that sinking feeling when I realised that there was nothing more I could do to 'fix it'. I felt physically ill and my body begged me to stop. At that point, I struggled to sleep, suffered anxiety attacks, and piled on weight. I realised that the price I was paying was too high; my relationships with the people I love were at breaking point. I was at breaking point. I faced my biggest fear and left. It frazzles me that there is such an enormous emphasis on the importance of mental health in the workplace, but that workplace bullying, one of* *the biggest root causes – in my opinion anyway – is still largely swept under the carpet. The silent epidemic in today's global business landscape.* **Marilise de Villiers, Founder & CEO, Marilise de Villiers Basson Consulting Ltd**

"...In my experience the majority of people do not come to work to deliberately bully or harass others, good people can easily find themselves in bad situations and a quick reminder that we all typically have good intentions and can 'rise up' sometimes help lift everyone. It amazes me how easily our desire to make an impact, be noticed, be vital, and make a difference can unintentionally negatively impact others, being open and respectful of other peoples 'truth' is important in getting back to a calm and positive working environment where possibilities are the norm..." **Andy Woodfield, Partner, Chief Sales and Marketing Officer at PwC UK**

Consultation Packages

*"The most important investment you
can make is in yourself."*
~ Warren Buffett ~

Wilson Hinds Consulting Ltd offers a series of developmental workshops and coaching initiatives synergised with the concept and principles of Emotional & Cultural Intelligence, using the EQ-i 2.0/EQ 360® and Emotional Intelligence Skills Assessment Profile (EISAP 2.0) assessments; allowing individuals to explore and understand the key principles of emotional and cultural intelligence, enabling them to Realise, Unlock and Release their Potential to be the best that they can be within their own job roles and specialisms.

We provide an excellent standard of service on an equitable learning platform, with accredited facilitators and coaches, who will be disseminating a wealth of experience spanning over 30 years'; which will provide you with the tools and resources you need to develop further along your career or life pathway whether starting out in the world of work, aspiring leaders or senior leaders; workshops are tailored to clients' needs and organisational requirements.

For a bespoke package to suit your organisational, leadership and workforce needs without busting your budget, please contact us via:

Email: information@wilsonhindsconsulting.com
Website: www.wilsonhindsconsulting.com
Twitter: @ReleasingYou

Offerings:

- The **EQ** Leadership Formula™ Coaching Programme

- Exploring Emotional & Cultural Intelligence – Using Emotional Intelligence Skills Assessment Profile (EISAP 2.0)

- **Tools for Success:** Emotional Resilience & Wellbeing within the Workplace

- The Equality & Inclusion Champions (EQI) Programme

- **Journey to Empowerment:** *Women's Transformational Leadership Programme*

Collaborations:

- **Synergised Solutions: Transforming Bias:** *From Unconscious to Conscious* - 3-Day Modular Change Programme info@synergisedsolutions.com